The Miseducation of the Privileged

By Nash

Table of Contents

“Can you just wait until we get there to text? You’re starting to Swerve!” I was driving fine but apparently my husband woke up today with the idea that he was my parent and not my partner.” Hmm I don’t know; can you get off my case and stop treating me like a child?”

“I am not treating you like a child but I would like to get there in one piece.”

“With you talking to me, I will be missing a piece of my mind by the time we…”

PSHHHH* *SCRREEEEEECCH* *BOOM

Airbags deployed on both sides of the car, splattering the shattered glass from the windows with dust. Feelings of regret blanketed the area for blocks, as bystanders could hear the mental screams, “I knew I should have driven”, but it was far too late for should haves. The car, once worth half a million dollars, now mimicked a python, as it wrapped around its prey, a pole, sucking the life out of everything that surrounded it. The bottom of the pole spilled signs of pain, as red rain lined the pavement.

“Oh, my God, what happened? Taylor, are you ok?”

That was the first sentence that I was able to make speak. The panic in Sebastian’s voice was making his words barely understandable. I groggily mumbled, “I’m fine. Are you ok?”

“Yeah just a little shaken up, but how does the car look?”

“I do not know but I will go check.” The sounds of the sirens disrupted and quickly ended all of the conversation. There must have been a patrol car patrolling close enough to hear the crash because no one had gotten the chance to find our phone, let alone dial 911. Two officers got out of their car and walked around it, surveying the extent of the damages. One of the officers stopped at the hood of our car and the color immediately faded from his face. He must have realized it was an expensive car; seeing it like this made me sick as well. He walked away and muscled the stomach to make a call over his radio.

"We have a 4 and 53, code 5."

I had no idea what the numbers meant, but I knew that we were ok and they did not need to call for backup. Honestly, they could leave; we would call the insurance company ourselves and get a rental sent immediately.

"Officers, we are all ok and I will pay for the damages to the pole."

He sternly replied, "Ma'am, I'm afraid you are going to have to pay for more than just the damages to the property."

My confusion could be heard clear as day in my speech, "What do you mean? What else do I have to pay for?" If his stern tone was not frightening enough, it had now transformed into

a serious authoritative one. I started to get out of the car to talk with him face to face. As I opened the door, the officer yelled at me.

"Ma'am, stay in the car! Put your hands on the steering wheel!"

I had no idea why he would not allow me to get out of the car. "Sir, you do not need to yell at me. Why can't I get out of my car?"

"Ma'am, there was a man sitting on this corner, but he is now lying under your car."

I did not recall seeing a man sitting there but if he was, he is clearly not someone beneficial to society. "So are you here to thank me?"

"Thank you? THANK YOU?" The officer's authoritative tone was now pure anger.

"Ma'am why would I thank you for this?"

"Well I kind of did your job for you. Homeless people infect the streets and bring down property values. More than likely, he was robbing innocent people every day so it's honestly like a two for one deal."

Silence fell upon our conversation and I could tell that he did not agree with my idea of this man's value. I began offering solutions. "So, you want me to pay for his funeral? Do homeless people even have funerals? I mean, like, who would really miss him?" That was not the answer that he was looking for and in less than a minute he had managed to grab his cuffs and move from standing in front of my car to standing right beside the driver's side.

"The ambulance is on its way; I am going to ride with you to the hospital, " he commanded sternly.

"A police escort to the hospital, why would I need that?"

"Because you are a murderer and murderers get police escorts to the hospital."

Murderer? That word sounds so filthy and lower class. I am not a murderer. As I observed the officer a bit closer, I could almost see why he would use such words to describe me. By his slouched posture and his barely graduated from the academy demeanor, it was hard to imagine him using any further developed language or vocabulary. By the way he was speaking to me it was clear his access to news outlets was limited to social media posts and that he had no idea to whom he was speaking.

“Do you know who I am? My husband could buy and sell your simple existence until he got tired.”

His tone indicated he was now extremely annoyed, so I knew there was no chance he would be letting me go to the hospital by myself.

“That might be true but once you are cleared by a doctor you are going to jail. And until he decides to pay your bail, if the judge allows it, your husband will be seeing you behind bars. I’m not going to ask again.”

Arguing with him was literally starting to kill my brain cells, so to end the torture of hearing him speak, I put my hands behind my back. “Sebastian, call my lawyer and he better beat me to the hospital!”

The ambulance arrived, and just as he said, the officer rode in the back with me. When we arrived at the hospital, he paraded me down the halls. If the handcuffs weren’t enough, the mere image of being escorted by a police officer, was humiliating enough. What were people thinking? I would be thinking the worse had I seen someone in my situation. Only true criminals are deserving of such treatment. I was no criminal.

Chapter One

I was furious at the judge's decision! What is the point of paying him if he is still going to punish me? My husband didn't seem too bothered by the news, but then again, he wasn't the one that had to deal with it. At the very least he was going to hear how I felt. "A year working with these speed bumps! Can you believe that the judge gave me a year? A whole year to work with a bunch of homeless losers." Each word came out like a fire ball of confusion and disbelief.

"Taylor, he gave you a year to be a volunteer homeless shelter counselor. He could have sentenced you to life for murder. Even on good behavior you would not be out until you were your father's age."

I hated it when he mentioned my father and he knew that. The calm demeanor in which Sebastian was speaking only added fuel to my anger. "How can they even be mad? It's like I did them a favor getting one of those abominations off of the streets. I should be getting an award for doing the officer's job."

"You killed a guy last night because you wanted to text instead of pay attention to the road. And if that wasn't enough, you already had more than your share of wine at the restaurant. I told you that I should drive, but oh no. No one can drive your car, not even the man who paid for it. The only thing saving you from being behind bars is the fact that I threw enough money at the judge to make it disappear."

"So, is this where you tell me I told you so? I have to live in hell for a year, but oh you're right, All Hail King Sebastian and his money! If the guy actually cared about his life, he wouldn't have been homeless; now would he? There are tons of jobs out there just waiting but instead of applying to them, these people decide to beg on the streets. And I should feel bad that I didn't see one at night? It was dark, he was dark, and if he believed that his own life was worth anything he would not have been sleeping on the curb."

"Oh, like the job you have Taylor? Maybe you could have gotten him work at the same place you go everyday to earn a living. I don't think you could be any more ungrateful if you tried. You didn't know the guy. He could have been trying to find work and not had any luck. You have always been well off so you wouldn't even understand being that low."

His tone was so condescending that I could not hold back any longer. If he wanted me to be this ungrateful bitch, then that is exactly what I would be. "So, I should apologize for my father being wealthy? I should apologize for not growing up in the trailer park like you and gaining all of your '*street cred*'? You found a way out and did quite well for yourself. You're a millionaire, and well you managed to marry me."

"No Taylor. You shouldn't apologize for growing up in a privileged lifestyle. You shouldn't even apologize for your thoughts towards the homeless. What you should apologize for is being a heartless bitch who feels like the world should bend over and kiss the ground she walks on."

"Well, well, well, Sebastian just tell me how you really feel. Well you know what, this bitch has to get ready to go down to scum city and pretend to listen to its occupants for the next five hours. Oh, and this bitch will be sleeping in the bed alone tonight since her husband wants to defend people he doesn't even know, INSTEAD OF HIS WIFE!" I could tell that Sebastian was frustrated with the conversation by the way he shook his head.

"That's just fine by me Taylor."

"Oh, I'm so glad. Goodbye Sebastian!" I slammed the door and with great hesitation I was off to start the worst year of my life.

Chapter Two

I barely had both of my feet inside of the shelter before the stench of low self-esteem and utter mediocrity invaded my nostrils. The odor was the equivalent of a six-hundred-pound woman who had not bathed or even moved in months, or a gallon of milk that had been sitting in the desert sun for a week. The worst part about it was that you could not get away from the smell. I could feel the stench enter my body through my nose and mouth and quickly spread to infect my lungs and abdomen. I prayed that I would be able to scrub the scent of poverty from my skin once I made it home.

My discomfort was interrupted by a woman walking up to me with her hand out. She introduced herself as Miss Green but the only thing my mind could focus on was why she would actually choose to be here. I know that it could not be for the paycheck because if they could not afford to eat, how in the hell could they afford to pay her?

"Good afternoon, I am Lily Green. You must be Mrs. Thomas."

"Actually, it is Dr. Thomas." I did not work my ass off with school and muscling through late night extra credit sessions with my sociology professor to be referred to as Mrs. If I did not want to be referred to as a doctor, I never would have gone down on him. At that point, I had missed so many of his classes because I was hungover or jetlagged that it was either suck his uncircumcised wrinkly penis and get an A, or repeat the class. And honestly right now, with my so-called husband conducting himself in the manner in which he did earlier, I might not even be a Mrs. for much longer. I still cannot believe the things that he said to me. He knew the type of person I was before he asked me to marry him and I never showcased the desire or willingness to change that. My mind was all over the place today, anything to disassociate my body with the hell I just walked in to.

"My apologies, Dr. Thomas."

I was trying my best to listen to what she was saying but my attention was clearly diverted. I was able to table my conversation with Sebastian in my head and focus my energy on surveying the room. I did not see a metal detector at the front of the building. What if one of these people brought in a weapon and attacked me? This might actually end up being worse than jail. At least in jail I could sell a few cartons of cigarettes to a manly woman named Bertha for my protection. I imagine it would not be much different from the movies. I am surprised that they are allowed to smoke. Does the idea of dangerous inmates having access to fire not bother anyone but me?

"Dr. Thomas, Dr. Thomas did you hear me?"

"My apologies, I am still trying to get used to the smell. You were saying?"

"I'm not sure what smell you're referring to, but I asked if you wanted a tour of the facility.

How could she not be sure of the smell that I was referring to? If poverty and depression had an odor and that odor could be paired with pure laziness and transformed into a cologne, it

I would still smell a bit better than this place. And a tour? She could not be serious. What was there to really see in a place like this? Four walls and dirty scum bags, what else was there to show? "Are the homeless people in here right now?"

"Umm yes ma'am. We offer college classes and run a daycare center so someone is pretty much always here."

The only thing that bothered me more than the homeless was their choice to reproduce. If you want to have a shitty life than by all means, do so, but do not force that life onto your children. If you are homeless you should be mandated to put your children up for adoption so they can have the chance of a better life. "Well I do not want to interrupt anyone, so how about you just take me to where I will be hosting the counseling sessions."

"Of course, Dr. Thomas. Right this way."

The walls were a pale peach color and full of frames in an attempt to make the place look like a home. It failed tremendously. What is the point of having a homeless shelter look like a home, if in the morning they would just be kicked back out on the streets? Some may think that the chips in the walls added character but, in actuality, they were doors for vermin to enter the building. That is besides the vermin that entered through the front door. They probably welcome four legged rodents right along with the two legged ones. We passed several bedrooms on the

way to the therapy office; they almost looked like dorm rooms for normal college students. They had what appeared to be clean linen on the beds, dressers, closets, mirrors, and desks. There was not anything with much street value, but the fact that everything was still intact and presentable was a surprise.

It felt like we had been walking for hours, but when I glanced down at my watch not even a minute had passed. Was this how things would feel here for a year? If seconds already felt like hours, there is no way that I would be able to do a year here before going insane myself. As I refocused my attention to following Miss Green, I noticed her ID badge. It read Lily Green, Ph.D. Even more confusing than her working here, was why she did not introduce herself as a doctor. I completed ten years of college for my doctorate so I always introduce myself as doctor.

"Excuse me Miss Green. Could I ask you another question?"

"Of course, Dr. Thomas, how may I help you?"

"Your badge lists that you have your Ph.D. Why did you not introduce yourself as a doctor especially after learning that I was one as well?"

"Well Dr. Thomas, if it's one thing that I have learned while working here, it's not to get too caught up with labels. You'll see that people from different academic and cultural backgrounds have ended up here. No matter how many degrees you have on the wall or how much money you have in the bank, when life wants to screw you, it just bends you over; no warning, no questions asked, and no sympathy."

"Even if you believe that, you have your doctorate. Why are you a secretary in a dump like this?"

"What makes you think that I am a secretary?"

"Well, you are the one that greeted me at the door, and the one offering me tours. That is the work of a secretary."

"Dr. Thomas, are you aware of the consequences of assuming?"

It was clear to me what she was hinting. Who does she think she is to insult me in such a manner?

"That is a pretty grand assessment for someone who probably got her doctorate out of a cereal box. I doubt your school has accreditation, so even with a high degree from the Scum Academy, you could only land a job where your only competition is high school dropouts and ex cons."

"My grandfather always told me that assuming only makes an ass out of you and me."

"Oh wow. Sounds like he was a doctor just like you."

Lily's calm demeanor reminded me of Sebastian and it fueled my overall frustration in being here. I wanted her to get upset so that I could have an excuse to walk out of this dump and never look back.

"No. He was actually a captain in the Marines."

Lily's response surprised me, torpedoing me back into my current hell. "I am sure he was quite disappointed that you ended up here."

"Contrary to your assumptions, he could not have been prouder of me. You see Dr. Thomas, I am not the secretary here. I am the owner and sole investor of this shelter. Every wall, couch, bed, and crumb that you see in this place was paid for from my personal account."

I glanced over her outfit again. She was wearing what resembled a grey sack that failed at its attempt to become a dress, and a pair of Mary Jane's where the heel was so low you could mistake them for tap shoes.

"Well you do not smell like money, so when did you win the lottery or rob the bank?"

"I did none of the above, but I did become an instant millionaire."

"How is that?"

"The thesis that I completed for my doctorate contained a theory that was adopted by doctors around the country, and the successful completion of my therapy practices has lowered violence, suicide rates, teen pregnancy rates, and unemployment in the inner cities. I would say that I am surprised that you have never heard of my work since it's been published in psychology magazines and the front of newspapers around the world, but you seem like a bubble woman, closed off from any part of the world that doesn't take a MasterCard. I'm sure that you haven't

opened many books without the word check in front of it since you obtained your doctorate. Now I would love to stay and talk, but I have a meeting with my accountant and you have a meeting with the group. Now if you will excuse me. Enjoy your day, Dr. Thomas."

"Miss Green."

I watched as she walked away. I could not believe that she had spoken to me that way and I would definitely tell my husband about the blatant disrespect. He may not have agreed with the way I felt about working here, but he would still defend my right to have those feelings. The knob to the therapy room door felt like ice in my hand. I prayed that I remembered to bring my hand sanitizer with me. My purse was safely locked away in my car but at least I would have easy access to it to rub off the stench of this place. I felt like I would need to bathe in bleach after leaving here. I could hear the rats conversing inside, probably trading robbery tactics or their drug dealers' numbers. My skin crawled and my stomach turned, but it was time to get started. Here goes day one.

"Hello, I am Dr. Thomas and I will be your new group therapist."

"Nice to meet you Dr. Thomas, I'm Francesca."

Francesca was in a dingy white t-shirt and jeans that clearly came from the clearance rack at a flea market. I could see slight residue from whichever soup kitchen meal she had for lunch. Her hair was long and wavy but the beauty of it was hidden in the ponytail held together by a rubber band. Her nails were in desperate need of a manicure, which made the idea of what

her feet must look like, almost unbearable. She stood there with her hand out expecting me to grab it and shake but she couldn't really be serious. . .could she? I was in a thousand-dollar suit and $500 pumps; did she really think I would touch her?

"Hmm guess you're not the hands-on type? Let me guess; too afraid that you'll catch the poor?

Francesca chuckled as though she was joking, but she was right. I knew in my mind that I would not "catch the poor," as she put it, but I did not want to take any chances.

"I got news for you baby, it don't work that way."

"I am not your baby. As I stated before, I am Dr. Thomas, your new group therapist." She chuckled again. I could tell then that this was going to be one long year. Her sarcastic joy desecrated my ears.

"Oh, you won't last here long."

"I wish. Unfortunately, I will be here for a year."

"Frannie that's the psych they told us about. You know . . . the murderer. Thought that she could throw enough dead presidents to cover that dead body. Too bad for her, the judge couldn't let that happen, so he's punishing her by sticking her with the scum."

How rude of her! I had not been in the room for a full five minutes and the slander had already begun. I knew that someone would recognize me!

"And you are?"

"Oh, where are my manners? Let me introduce you to everyone. Of course you have met Francesca. The rest of the members of the group are James, little Lauren, Garrett, Craig, Naomi, and I am Tori. Nice to meet you."

Tori was more put together than Francesca; at least someone in here cared. She had straight black hair with blonde highlights cut into a bob. Tori had on jeans, a peach tank top, and a black blazer. If we were in a different situation, I may have even asked her where she got her cheetah print ballet flats from, but with her being in here, I am sure they were either stolen or given to her by a pimp. She had this arrogance about her that most probably have mistaken as confidence. Someone has fed her enough pointless information over the years for her to think that she knows it all and has it all figured out, but if that were true she would not be in the situation she is right now.

“How do you know about that Tori?”

“Oh Dr. Thomas there are no secrets in these walls.”

“So, I guess we can all sit down and you can tell me about your drug addictions and parentless children and after a year we can all go our separate way. I will be on my way to the Bahamas and you will go back to..well you all really do not have a place to go back to, do you, or does a cardboard box in a back-alley count?”

“Hmm, now is that the type of attitude that will keep your bougie ass out of jail? As I recall, if you can’t make it in here, then you’re off to jail for a year. You’re here to help us and you won’t even touch us. Like Frannie said, you won’t be here long.”

I hated the fact that she knew all of this information. As soon I get out of here I am calling my lawyer and making a case for breach of confidentiality and slander. She called me a murderer, but what I did could easily be synonymous to a butcher preparing meat. A simple means to an end; a necessity in a more enriching survival.

“Fine. We can help each other. You sit down and tell me about your lives, I pretend to listen, you all tell the judge I helped, and I’ll give you all $1000 bucks each.”

At this point, Francesca felt the need to chime in.

“You can’t just throw around your net worth and assume that it will solve all of your problems.”

She could not be serious. “You are homeless. What else could you possibly want besides money?”

"If money was all I cared about, I would have never become homeless."

"Explain."

Tori interrupted, yet again.

"Oh, it won't be that easy. We aren't going to just trust you with our stories. You are a money hunger narcissist. I would hate to see our lives be the source of your next paycheck."

"I see this is going to be a long year."

"You damn skippy doc."

Chapter Three

A hot shower after being in that dump was the closest thing to heaven I had experienced in a long time. I should have stayed to find out how the degenerates were able to learn my story, but no one bothered to give me a single file on them. I didn't even know all their names. There are seven people in the group and I only know two of their names. They must be the official welcome team… well at least Francesca. Tori just seemed like she wanted to get close enough to me to see what she could rob me for. I knew it was a good idea not to wear jewelry in that place.

I wanted to tell Sebastian about my first day but he was gone when I got home and hadn't come home by the time I woke up in the morning. I guess that as his wife I should be upset at that fact but I was slightly relieved. The tension between us had started to die down but I knew he was only trying to get back on my good side for one reason.

He has been dead set on having a baby soon and wanted to use our free time to make one. Not only was the sex subpar most days, I did not feel like getting fat just to make him happy. It is not like me getting pregnant is going to change his life at all. He would not be the one giving up wine for nine months or going through buttons popping and stretch marks. The whole idea of getting pregnant made my stomach turn, and that is why I am still taking my birth control pills. He thinks that things will just happen at the right time if we try hard enough but I like having insurance that it will never be the right time.

I used to be able to fake it through sex with him with ease but once we were married I did not see the need to fake anymore. There is no prenup, so whenever he feels the need to walk out of the relationship he is more than happy to walk. Now where he would find someone like me, I do not know but with half of his fortune in my bank account that would be the least of my worries. I would be too busy deciding on which country to fly to next. I was either going to get there with him or without him; it did not matter to me.

I was headed out the door when Sebastian finally decided to come home. He swung the door open as if something was chasing him, almost knocking me out. “Sebastian.”

“Hello Taylor.”

“How was your day?”

“Nice to see that the silent treatment is over. My day was just fine. How was your first day at the shelter?”

“Well since you finally asked, it was horrible.”

“Why was it horrible Tay?”

He was monotone and it was obvious that he lacked sincere interest about my response; he just wanted to be able to say that he asked. At this point it didn’t matter if he actually cared, I just wanted to get my experience out of my system. Friends were a scarcity for me so he was my only outlet.

“Well the building itself smelled like sin and pig sex.”

“When have you ever smelled pig sex?”

"Well, I haven't but with them being filthy animals I imagine that it wouldn't be a pleasant experience. But that's not the point. The point is that I spent most of the time praying for an oxygen mask, and the rest of it wishing that the hands on the clock would speed up."

"How were the people?"

People he calls them. What low standards he must have for human life. A pile of flesh just needed a pulse for Sebastian to deem their existence relevant. "They're homeless, how do you think they were? I am just glad that they clearly had all taken their meds and were able to maintain human qualities for my time there. There was this one obnoxious woman who somehow decided she was close enough to a normal human being to talk to me without being given permission. Oh, and when I walked into the therapy room this woman named Francesca actually thought I would shake her hand. I could tell by her lack of manicure that she did not care enough about herself to keep herself up."

"You know Taylor, I would say I cannot believe the disrespect that is forming and spilling out of your mouth and resembling a rabies induced seizure, but I would be lying."

"Look, I am who I am and I'm not afraid to show it, which is more than I can say for you. You might be able to fool the world, but let's not forget the real reason you asked me to marry you."

"Everyone has secrets; unfortunately, there are some truths worse than the secrets. You want a pat on the back for not hiding who you are, but there's nothing about you that's celebratory. You're an awful person and if I knew then what I know now, this union would have never happened. You bring out the worst in everyone that crosses your path."

"Oh, I am so sorry that I can't be Saint Sebastian, the defender of the poor because he had to live in a double wide instead of a mansion! Sebastian, you are damn near a billionaire; it's time to stop playing the victim role."

"That is where you have always been wrong. I am not a victim. I just happened to have a different upbringing than you. Instead of boarding passes, I had a bus pass and you can't make me ashamed of that. In my thirty-two years of life I've grown from that double wide to this mansion that you come home to every night. In your life, you've just shuffled from place to place. And even though those places are cased in expensive monetary possessions, if the owner of those things decided that you weren't welcome to enjoy them anymore, you would have nothing. The only thing I am ashamed of is that I loved the person I thought you were, the mask."

"I won't apologize for being beautiful. Just like my bank account, I was gifted with this at birth."

"The fact that you assume I am referring to your physical features is just proof. Once upon a time you would come out with me in your jeans and t-shirt to feed the ducks at the pond. We would walk the strip and eat at places that served food on a stick. What happened to that Taylor?"

"You didn't fall for me; you fell for the character I played. I needed a wealthy husband and you needed a beautiful woman inside and out. The outside part was easy but I actually had to force myself to do some of the things we did. Volunteer at an animal shelter? Please! The only thing I love with fur is hanging in my closet. And if you hate me so much, why are we still married?"

"You know damn well why. A divorce voids the confidentiality agreement you signed. The preservation of my secrets is more important than my happiness right now. In due time."

"Exactly. You need me as much as I need you, so get over the saint act. Now if you don't mind, I'm running late. Maybe you can come down to the shelter and find a better suitor."

"Goodbye Taylor."

"Sebastian."

Chapter Four

"Good morning Dr. Thomas."

"Lily."

I could not believe I was in this hell hole yet another day. I tried to settle my stomach by reminding myself that 360 days is less than 365, but it was no help. Every minute I spent slumming, felt like I was replaying my worst nightmare. My worst nightmare is being poor, so I guess it made sense why this environment would amplify it.

"I have to say I am surprised to see you back; I was sure that the group would send you running."

"It is going to take more than the silent treatment to send me running."

"The silent treatment?" Lily chuckled. I would bet good money that this place had a gas leak as much as everyone laughs here. It is not like their lives had any joy in them that would incite laughter. "Oh, that is going to be heavenly once they start talking. You still look at them as obstacles in your way to freedom. When those "things" start showing you their humanity you are going to be in for a rude awakening."

"I highly doubt that. You and I are people. We work for what we want and have the proof to show for it. Those monstrosities in the back room are not people."

"Do not be so quick to judge; you might see you have more in common with them than you wish to believe."

"Well since you chose to blatantly disrespect me with that last little statement, I think this conversation is officially over. You have a good day Lily."

"You do the same Dr. Thomas."

How dare she say that? She continues to disrespect me like I live here or even voluntarily work here. I can see why the hourly residents act the way that they do and say the things they say. I guess it's time for day five in this hell hole. As if my day was not already off to a great start, Tori was the first person to notice me walking into the room.

"Oh, look who made it back again. I have to admit, I didn't think you would."

"It seems like that feeling is unanimous with you people."

"You people? What do you mean by that?"

Francesca must have heard Tori's voice rising because she came over and kind of stood in between the two of us. I assumed she would simply pull Tori aside but she turned to face me.

"Hey doc I hate to break it to you, but you might find yourself having a lot in common with "*us people.*"

Again, with this? Did I smell poor today? Maybe my $400 frames made me look uneducated. Maybe I should wear some of my jewels to this place just to further perpetuate the fact that I am better than them. "I highly doubt that."

Francesca shook her head."Sit down, and get comfortable."

"And why on earth would I do that?"

"Because I have decided that telling you my story will be a lot more satisfying than not telling you my story."

"More satisfying for whom exactly?"

"You vacation on islands that my ex-husband owns and shop in boutiques that I once held stock in. You wear diamonds mined from my coal and the celebrities that you shake hands with were once on my speed dial. The mansion you drive home to every night could probably fit into the nanny's wing in my old house. Doc, you walk around here flaunting your riches, but I too had wealth. I had connections. I had power. My life was once a fairytale completed with my very own Prince Charming. You, you could not have even been a frog in my old life."

FRANCESCA

At age eighteen, I met the love of my life… the very subject of my soul. I know it may be difficult to believe that, but he stood there as my truth embodied in a human and I had no doubts. He was a college sophomore at one of the nearby colleges and looked like a Monday man. You see everyone knows God worked for six days and rested on the seventh, so by his next day working, Monday, he was well refreshed and creating at his best. He had a confidence that overflowed from his pores and gave a little to anyone in his presence. My ex-husband stood there exhibiting nothing short of a miracle.

I was immediately entrapped by him as he erased every doubt I had about life. Even the traits in him that I vowed to avoid, gleamed like the foreheads of children at a July cookout. I stood there, newly intoxicated, as he forcefully removed every possibility of getting things wrong. He walked up to me and told me to be ready at 7 p.m. Confused, yet excited, I questioned what he meant by that. He told me that was the time to which I needed to be ready. I asked him, what exactly did I need to be ready for and he told me I needed to be ready for my last, *first* date. We exchanged contact information and I floated away to get ready for our date.

That first date sparked a classic Cinderella story for us. We both tripped over any insecurity or hesitation and fell hard enough to shake Texas. A bat right out of hell must have been chasing our love because we were married before my nineteenth birthday. There was nothing in the world or beyond that could come in between our love. Surprisingly, my family and his family, stood beside our decision to get married. That is everyone, except his mother. She believed I was only marrying her son because of his money and she did not hesitate to tell us what she thought.

"That woman is going to drag you to hell," "I can see the dollar signs in her eyes," "She'll drop you for a dick with more diamonds," were just a few of her lovely phrases. In all honesty, I felt like she was projecting her own guilt onto me. She married his dad around the time the company was taking off. His dad might not have had the money in the bank that he did when he died, but his mother could see that he would. She could smell a quarter at the bottom of a dumpster and instantly make out a plan to flip that quarter into a hundred dollars within minutes. It was a life tragedy that such a brilliant mind had gone to waste in such a small, evil, almost devilish creature.

For seven years we dealt with her the best way we knew how. I chose to simply avoid her at all costs and my husband would spend his time with her, defending my character. We would have separate holidays and if she came to town I would suddenly have a business conference for the weekend; it worked. She would always ask him the same question when she saw him, "you take out the trash yet son? The longer you wait the harder it is to make the stench go away." I never understood why she hated me so much. Thankfully, the love with my husband was strong enough to deal with her wrath. And then the day came that she wasn't strong enough to dish it out anymore.

He would come home from seeing his mom and tell me that she wasn't looking her best and that he thought she was getting sick. But I just brushed it off. Evil never dies; I could not have that much luck in life. December 14th. That was the day his mom had her first stroke, and although I wanted to check on her in the hospital, we decided that it wasn't the best time for me and his mom to talk. I stayed behind and he ran to her side. He stayed there until she was released a week later. We had never spent more than three days apart from each other since, well since ever really. When she was safely back home at her dungeon of evil, he was happy to still have his mother and I was happy to be getting my husband back. Unfortunately, what came home was less of my husband, and more of his mother.

There was no, "Honey I missed you." Instead I was greeted with a harsh, "Where is the vodka?" I didn't mind him wanting a drink; he'd been under a lot of stress lately. I mixed his favorite, vodka and cranberry. After about five seconds, he had downed his drink and demanded another one, but scolded me to hold the cranberry. I knew there was something wrong, but I kept telling myself the stress had obviously affected his manners, so I poured him another drink… then another… and then another. It wasn't until he was about three quarters into the bottle that he started to actually talk to me.

"She almost died Frannie. I tried to tell her stories as a distraction, but as she was on her death bed the only thing she could think about was me; well, about us and our not having children. She didn't want to die without seeing her first grandchild."

I told him we could try to have a baby after fashion week; I had to make sure everything went well. I walked away thinking we were in agreeance, but apparently he did not like that answer. He did not like that answer at all. I turned my back to him and headed back to the kitchen but before I could make it to the kitchen, I felt a strong pull on my head. Before I knew it, I was on the ground. He flipped me over and ripped my shirt open.

"My mother wants a grandchild now and you are going to give her one whether you like it or not."

He grabbed my arms and put them above my head. I was able to head butt him in the chest and get up. I made it to the stairs but he caught up with me and dragged me down. I felt every step as my face and body slammed against them. Once I reached the bottom of the staircase, he turned me around and slapped me on my face. I was dizzy, but I vividly remember cursing at myself. "Fuck! You did it again Frannie. You told yourself never again and then you fucked up." My husband was not the first man to raise his hand to me in a less than loving manner.

I touched my face. My mouth was bleeding. Weirdly, it distracted me from the throbbing my entire body was experiencing. I was able to get up and push him. I just wanted him to stop hitting me. He fell back and hit his head. There was a struggle and the next thing I remembered was waking up, still on the floor with dried blood on my lip and cheek. My clothes were ripped and tossed beside me. This was not him, he loves me. I knew what kind of men that hit women were like and my husband was not like that. It was just an accident in his drunken rage. We all make mistakes, so I forgave him.

As I headed upstairs to take a shower I heard the water running. I entered the bathroom and was greeted with a surprise. He had run a hot bubble bath for me and prepared a full breakfast of my favorites. How could I stay mad when he was clearly sorry? I enjoyed my meal and my bath before making love to him on the bathroom floor. This was a mistake that would never happen again. Besides, mistake or not, he was my husband. . . I loved him.

A few weeks passed and I could not stay out of the toilet. My period was late and the smell of food made me nauseous. I was pregnant. I called my husband and he happily rushed home from work and gave me the tightest, most fulfilling embrace I'd ever had. I could feel the sincerity of his love as he attempted to mold together all of my broken pieces.

We rushed to his mother's estate, only to be welcomed with sirens. Frantically, he rushed into the home he had been raised in to find the woman that raised him, cold. A second stroke had killed his mother. Just when things were getting better…they weren't.

On February 5th, we buried his mother. He was a rock through the wake and the funeral, but as soon as he got home, he crumbled. He curled up and cried on my stomach for what seemed like hours. And then, as though he was a robot and a switch was pushed, he lifted his head and wiped his eyes. The moment he turned to face me, I saw the coldest look in his eyes.

"This is your fault. If you had not been obsessed with your career, we could have had children years ago and my mother would not have stressed about dying before holding her first grandchild. You murdered my mother. You murdered my mother!"

When the last word left his mouth, the first slap landed on my face. Then, a punch to my chest. He dragged me down by my hair onto the floor and kicked me. I was two months pregnant with a child he wanted; but that did not matter at the moment. At that moment, I was not his wife or the mother of his unborn child. No, at that moment, I was a murderer and his mother was my victim.

That night I lost my baby. I could not pinpoint which blow released my child's soul or which one knocked me out. Thankfully, he was kind enough to take me to the hospital. I do not remember the EMT coming or arriving at the hospital, but when I finally came to, I could see he had filled the hospital room with flowers and balloons. The nurse commented on how lucky I was to have a husband who never left my side during such a horrific event. Apparently, I had been distraught about his mother and in a crying fit as I ran downstairs. Having missed a step, I tripped and stumbled down the remainder of the stairs. I went along with the lie because it was somewhat comforting. I would have rather fallen on the stairs than to have watched my husband fall from grace. He said he would never hurt me again, but he did just bury his mother. And afterall, he did just bury his mother. Mistake or not, he was my husband… I loved him.

After the miscarriage, I started to drift away from my husband and more towards my family. His mother was the last bit of family he had left, so he couldn't understand. We began to fight more and more about how I was spending my time. In my mind, I felt he would have another mistake soon and I would be left to explain it to my family…again. I was sure they wouldn't believe that I fell down the stairs two times in such a short time span.

Two years passed and he didn't have any more mistakes. It was like we were stupid teenagers again; just focused on our love. For our ten-year anniversary, he even booked a cruise to Jamaica. We had always talked about going, but there was always something more important that got in the way. But not this time. I'm not sure if it was the gentle rock of the boat or the margaritas that we constantly had delivered to our room, but we barely left the boat. For a week straight, we made love with no interruptions. We weren't back for two weeks before I found out I was pregnant again.

He was amazing this time around. We glided into my four-month check-up; it was time to find out the sex of the baby. He wanted a junior, of course, but I only cared about a healthy baby. "It's a girl!" I flashbacked to the last time he did not get his way, my heart stopped cold. I just knew he would have a fit and the fit would lead to another mistake…but he didn't. He was excited.

"I'm going to have a beautiful princess soon; better get the shotgun ready now if she looks at all like her mother. I'm going to be fighting fast little boys off until she's thirty." We giggled at the thought, finished up the visit, and headed home.

"I want to name her after my mother."

I should have known this was coming. I knew he loved his mother, but I just did not want my child named after a woman that hated me. I told him we could decide on a variation of his mother's name. He did not like that answer.

"So you stress my mother to death and now you can't even honor her through my child? You are such a selfish bitch! My mother was right, you probably just want to have this baby so you can leave me and take my money. Your plan won't work though! You hear me you dumb slut!! Your plan won't work if I have anything to do with it."

He beat me for over an hour and I counted every second of it. He was picking up anything in his reach to assist him and I was attempting to think of anything other than him attacking me. I must have passed out because I woke up in the hospital again; the same hospital I lost my first child two years ago. The doctor came in and asked me if I knew where I was. I answered that I did and he asked if I remembered how I got here. I told him that I slipped on a sock while doing laundry and fell down the stairs at my house. Somehow, I must have sounded convincing because he left the topic alone. He moved on to the topic of my baby.

She was dead. Internal bleeding had made sure of that. My daughter dying made the things my husband said true. I was a murderer. No, I did not hit myself in the stomach, but I stayed with a man that I knew was capable of hitting me in my stomach. My husband killed my first child, and by staying with him I indirectly gave him permission to do it again. In my heart, I knew better, but damn I loved my husband, and I was to hold true to my vows.

Losing my first child was bad enough. But now the baby that had made a home in my stomach, the baby that craved pepperoni pizza with peanut butter on top, the baby that kicked and moved, keeping me up at night. . . that baby was now dead inside of me. She was growing nicely and had gotten too big, so I had to have an emergency C section. I watched as my baby was cut out of me and placed on a dish. Her hands were closed in a fist like she was fighting to stay alive. Her mouth was open like she was screaming at me to help her. I could almost hear what her screams would have sounded like and the thought made me nauseous. That was my baby girl. Her father was worried about protecting her from boys and instead she died from his very own hands.

The loss of my daughter left me in a deep depression. I missed weeks of work and although my boss loved me, she could not continue to be understaffed. She fired me. What did I have now? My husband would come home after work and just have his way with me. I didn't care anymore. That night, I died along with my baby girl.

This went on for months and then I felt it again. The morning sickness, the cravings, the swelling; it was all back. I was pregnant. I was pregnant and I refused to stay around until another "mistake" happened. I carefully watched him get ready for work, even kissed him goodbye. As soon as his car disappeared from the neighborhood, I ran through the house grabbing clothes, food and the cash from the safe. I ran to my car realizing then that getting the car and it's insurance in my name was the smartest thing I had ever done. I sped away from the crime scene disguised as my home. My family disowned me after finding out the truth about my husband, so I didn't have anywhere to go. But I just knew I had to find a place to hide.. At least until I had my baby. Mistake or not, he was my husband. . . I loved him. But not more than I loved my baby.

March 5, 1999. I gave birth to a beautiful baby girl. Her name was Mariah Alexander and she was my perfect miracle baby. After paying for the medical bills and baby supplies, I was tapped out. My husband had cut me off completely once he saw that I left. But I didn't care because I didn't want my baby around him anyway. My only joy was that he did know about my recent pregnancy.

Mariah looked up at me one night when we were lying down together in the back seat of my car; at that moment, I knew she deserved way more than this. The next morning I drove to a car lot and sold my car for two thousand dollars. I put the cash in an envelope and found the nearest hospital. I walked into the maternity ward, placed Mariah and her diaper bag with the envelope peeking out, in the waiting room and walked away. I left a note stating her name, birthday, blood type, allergies, and that she was very much loved. It's been seventeen years since I've seen my baby girl and not a day goes by without me thinking of her. I can only hope that she is safe and happy.

After I left her in the hospital I went on to try to get a job and make something of myself. The plan was to hire a detective and track her done once I was stable. My plans didn't really go as I as I hoped. No one was hiring fashion assistants.

The days out of work turned into weeks, which turned into years. I would do odd jobs for a few months and then be out of work again. What you all see right now is me in between jobs. I'll find something new soon. I always do. And when I save enough money, I will find my daughter. She may hate me for leaving her, but I have to let her know I wanted nothing but the best for her. Mariah has my heart; she was and will forever be my reason for trying; my reason for living.

Chapter Four - Part Two

Everyone in the room fell silent. But, like clockwork, Tori had to talk.

"Damn Frannie. So, where's your kid now?"

"I wish I could tell you. I have been saving up every dime I've made to hire a private investigator to find her. Who knew it would take decades to save 20,000 dollars. I still have about 1,500 dollars left to save, but when I do, I'll find her. I'll find her and I'll explain everything. I'll tell her that I love her and that I always have. I'll tell her how I pray every day since that day, that she had ended up with a loving family who took care of her. I may have missed eighteen years, but I would spend the rest of my life with her if she allowed me."

She cannot really expect me to believe her story. "So, you became homeless to protect a child that you do not even have right now? How do you even know if she is still alive? You don't even know what type of person picked her up when you walked away."

"You're right doc, I don't. What I do know is she had a fighting chance and that's more than I can say if I would have stayed with her father. She would've just been another mistake to him. I might not be perfect but at least I gave my kid a shot. I was able to keep her safe enough to take her first breath and say her first word. It may not seem like much to you doc, but it was more than I was able to do for her siblings."

"Did you have any other kids after her? Are there other hospitals with unclaimed children in their maternity ward?"

"No. Mariah was my miracle baby because the doctor told me after my 2nd miscarriage that trying to get pregnant again would be a waste. He said I clearly was not in a situation that prompted a healthy pregnancy. He was right. You might not understand it, but then again, I'm not asking you to understand. The only forgiveness I need is from God and Mariah Alexander. God forgave me long ago; now I just have to find my daughter."

"It is clear even if we were somehow once in the same world, we have never shared the same vision. If I wanted something to take care of I would have gotten a puppy. Your husband can't beat a puppy out of you and it's so less trying on the body. Happy husbands write checks. You're evidence of what an unhappy one does."

"I cannot even judge you for your perspective on this."

"Judge me? How could you even begin to judge me? My husband would never put his hands on me the way that yours did. Even if he did, it would not have taken me two miscarriages and hospital visits to leave him."

"My husband would not have put his hands on me either. My husband, the man that I married, was perfection. He was everything to me and I gratefully placed him on a pedestal that extended to the heavens. It literally took him crashing down and burning from that pedestal for me to realize how much I had lowered my self-worth to match the way he made me feel. He belittled me to nothing more than a punching bag and a ghost day care. Yet, I continued to make excuses for him. I wondered what type of corruption sorcery I must have had in order to transform my king into my terrorizer. It was me. For years, it was me and I could not even think of myself as a woman in an abusive relationship. I had no doubts that I was abused in my previous relationship because my boyfriend looked like an abusive person. He fit the mold of someone who would hit their woman. But my husband shattered that mold. My husband forced me to reconsider my view of fear. It was no longer a stranger in a hoodie attempting to sell me merchandise from the back of his car. Now I look at fear as the clean cut, well-dressed man that attends appreciation balls. I learned there is no true representation for fear and you're much better off learning about someone pass their preserved image and net worth."

"There is nothing to learn beyond someone's net worth."

"So, you would condemn your soul to Hell for a few lousy bucks?"

"Condemn my soul to Hell? I vacation there."

"You are still going to stand here with the misconception that what happened to me could not happen to you?."

"Well it couldn't. My husband would never beat me. I don't even like kids. His parents love me. And, I have more than a car in my name."

"He might not hit you sweetheart, but every man has a secret. Every man."

Chapter Five

I could not wait to get home today. I can handle having to be around them for a year, but to think that I could possibly have anything in common with them, is horrifying. I am a debutante, a queen in the midst of jokers. I walked into my punishment knowing that they would not provide anything, but mere entertainment, and that woman wants me to believe that we are equals. That we were ever equals, is mind blowing. Who's to say she is not just lying? She never even said her so called "wealthy husband's" name. I bet she was never married, never had a dime to her name and never had kids. It is quite possible that she is just some quack off her meds. She did make one good point though… every man has a secret.

"Tay, you home?"

I must have been completely wrapped in reflection, because I didn't even hear Sebastian get home.

"In the kitchen."

"How are you doing today my love?"

"Well and yourself?"

"Amazing. You know how I have been waiting for my assistant to get back from break? Well school is back in session, which means he is back at work. I can breathe again."

"Sounds like you really missed him being there."

"I have. I never knew how much I needed the extra help around the office until I didn't have it anymore."

"You could have asked me for help; I would have filled in."

"Oh, I didn't want to bother you baby. I know you are busy at the shelter and it's stressing you enough. You don't need my extra stress weighing you down. Speaking of the shelter, how was it today?"

"It was better. They actually spoke to me today, but I'm not sure which one I prefer yet… the silence or the interaction."

"Well personally I enjoy the interaction I have at work. I couldn't imagine being around people and not conversing with them. You know how much I hate it when you get mad at me and give me the silent treatment."

"I know baby. We might not be the most perfect couple in history, but we still know how to get under each other's skin. That may not be the best thing, but it's proof that we know each other pretty well." "You might be right. I am going to go run a bath, should I leave the door open?"

"Tempting Tay, very tempting, but I can't tonight. I brought home my work tonight and I have to finish crunching these numbers for the new budget. The more money I save, the more money you can spend."

"Well since you put it that way, how can I be upset? Next time."

"Next time."

Chapter Six

I fear that this place is becoming familiar. It has only been a week and the odor from this place has attached itself to me. I can scrub my hair until my scalp is raw, yet the smell is still there. A stranger on the streets might even mistake me for one of them. That idea made me nauseous. Francesca's little bedtime story did not help with my fear of such misconception.

"Good morning Dr. Thomas."

"Miss Green."

"How are you doing today?"

"I am well and yourself?"

"Doing fine. I'm walking and I'm breathing. What could I complain about?"

"Well you have your PhD and you work with the trash. I complain about it every day and for me it is temporary."

"I work here by choice to help people. I'm not sure how I could explain it to you any better."

" You could have chosen to help a different group of people; cleaner, less painful on the eyes to look at."

"Do you mind if I ask you a question?"

"In need of advice? I am here to help."

"No, I don't need any advice. Why do you hate them so much?"

"And by them you are referring to?"

"The human beings who might be down on their luck, but still deserve to be treated like people."

"Oh, the walking waste of taxpayers' money. Well they usually smell awful, attack me when I walk down the street, and beg. I cannot stand someone who begs for things they could easily work to attain. There are plenty of jobs out there, but oh they do not want to work for a living; they would rather bother hard working people until they get enough change to buy their next fix."

"I really hate to burst your bubble but no one chooses to be homeless. These people are doing the best they can with the hands they are dealt. There might be jobs out there but who is going to hire someone that comes in to apply with no resume, no business attire, and the lowest of self-esteems that anyone could have? A lot of them have the skills and knowledge to do the job better than the next man, but they never get the chance to show that."

"Well young woman, I love to burst your bubble. There is someone in your shelter right now that chose to be homeless."

"Please, enlighten me. Who in this shelter do you feel chose to be homeless?"

"Francesca."

"Frannie? She didn't choose to be homeless. She chose to live and give her unborn child the opportunity to do the same. She gave every bit of money and energy she had to her child and has not seen her since she left her at that hospital. Do you have children?"

"God no. Children cost too much money and require too much energy. Plus, have you seen my body? I did not spend the money I did just to ruin it by having a child."

"That explains your reaction. But a piece of Frannie died that day. Life in a big mansion doesn't beat living."

"Of course you can say that now, you're rich."

"Dr. Thomas, unlike you I wasn't born into this life. My parents died when I was fifteen and I had no one. They were renting the house and their cars, so once the money ran out, the government came and took it all. I paid a store clerk to pose as my guardian so that the state wouldn't throw me into a foster home. I graduated high school homeless and alone, but at the top of my class. My break didn't come until I was offered a scholarship to a good college. I worked my ass off at a restaurant when I wasn't studying and I graduated college at the top of my class. You ask why I chose to help "these people." Well, the simple answer to your question is that '*these people*', are my people. If I can't help someone in a situation that I've been in, then what is the point of being rich?"

"Trips, clothes, diamonds, shoes... Shall I continue?"

"The fact that you didn't list shelter, water, or food, lets me know that you will never get it."

"I am not here to get it. I am here to do my time and get out."

"By all means; please do."

Nash

I should have known! Why else would a young woman with the highest degree you can get, work in a place like this. She could try to fool everyone else with her whole '*help the people'* speech, but not me. She is just like the rest of these t*hings* in here.

"She's back everybody! Who said that she wouldn't make it to day three? Pay up."

"You all were betting on if I would make it three days? Really?"

"We have to find some type of enjoyment in your being here."

"Excuse me, but what was your name again?"

"Craig."

Craig looked young. He could not have been more than twenty-three years old, but his eyes... His eyes had deep circles like he had seen too much too soon in his life. He was wearing burgundy jeans with a tight white button down. He had a royal blue bowtie and if I did not see him in here, I would just think he was some college student. His short wavy hair would fall and cover his eyes when he spoke, but they could not hide his piercing hazel eyes.

"Well hello sir."

"Oh honey if I was a sir, I wouldn't be homeless. I'm a queen baby, gawk at my crown and respect my castle."

"Quite some castle you got here."

"It's clean. I have people who love me for me, and I don't have to worry about being on the dl. This is a castle if my fairy ass has ever seen one."

“Well Ms. Craig while you are already flapping your gums, do you want to share your story so I can check another name off of my list?”

“Ooo sweetheart I thought you would never ask. I love being the center of attention. Gather around children, mama’s got a story to tell.”

CRAIG

I have four older sisters and my father was convinced that my mother could just not have a boy… that was until I came. My mother told me that they didn't even worry about the gender of the baby once she got pregnant with me, they knew that they would be having a fifth girl. They pulled everything out of the attic from when my sisters were first born and decorated the nursery once again. When the doctor pulled me out and told my parents, "It's a boy!" they told him to double check. They had to make sure that my penis wasn't just a piece of extra umbilical cord. My father said that once they finally accepted that I was a boy, all he could do was cry. Well, cry and insist that my mother bless him with a junior. She agreed that it is was time and she did just that. My father had a man that would allow his legacy to carry on. To the outside world, my father was my biggest and best support system. The reality wasn't so pretty.

I was your stereotypical little boy. I played video games on the weekends and I learned how to kick a ball before I learned how to walk. Once I could walk, I was catching the ball and by the time I was running I was throwing the ball better than kids twice my age. I did whatever I needed to do to be the son my father always wanted and when I would receive a MVP award I made sure that I thanked my father for pushing me.

From the outside looking in we had the perfect father-son relationship, but the reality was… my father hated me. I was the biggest disappointment for him because physically, I was the son he always wanted, but mentally I was wired wrong. I tried to fight it, I swear I did, but I couldn't help it. When I would shower after my games my eyes would shift. The water running down the bodies of some of my teammates, simply put, aroused me. I think my father suspected that I wasn't '*normal*' for a while, but as long as I played the role he was fine.

When I was about ten years old, my father caught me playing dress up with my sisters' clothes and make-up. The truth was officially out and there was no denying it anymore. He was supposed to be at work; he was never supposed to see me that way. I was doing what I always did when I was at home by myself; pretending that the hallway was my catwalk. I never thought he would see me like that, but when I got to the end of the stairs my father had reached the top of the stairs, and I will never forget the look in his eyes. His heart was broken by the sight of me. I could almost hear as each piece of it fell out of his chest and onto the floor.

As revenge for breaking his heart, he broke something of mine. Before I could even think of an excuse for the way I was dressed, he had already picked me up and thrown me down the stairs. I looked up, hoping that whatever trance he was in was over but it wasn't. My father came down to where I had fallen, picked me up, and slammed me against the wall. He broke my arm that day and when the pain became too much, and I wept from my soul, he threw me the phone. He said he would not further enable my journey to manhood by calling an ambulance for me. I was so embarrassed I didn't even call the ambulance. My father stormed out the house as I remained in the corner, clinging to my arm as if it were an Oscar.

I passed out, not waking up until my mother arrived home. I felt her touch my arm and I cringed as though I was some neglected animal. She took me to the hospital and forced my father to meet us there. When he came in the room I stared into his eyes as mine began to swell up with tears, just praying I would see an ounce of compassion or understanding in them. But there was none. His eyes were cold and still. It was at that moment I realized that not only had I broken his heart that day, but I lost him as well. For the rest of my life I would live without a father. No matter how many championships I won or how many girls I forced myself to sleep with, he would never see me as a man… not a real one at least.

"I have four daughters! Four daughters! I gave you my name and to repay me, you want to walk around looking like a bitch! How dare you!! There will be no fucking sissies living under my roof, so either stop or get the hell out!"

I was ten. I was ten when I found out my father would never love me for who I am. I didn't wake up the day before wanting to be comfortable in makeup and heels; that's just what happened. The only thing I was sure of was that boys were supposed to like girls and girls were supposed to like boys. When I got all dolled up and looked like a girl, it made it easier to accept the fact that I liked boys. I loved being a boy, it seemed a lot easier than being a girl but it was ok for girls to like boys; if I could just feel like a girl. My father would have never seen it that way, so I just had to make sure he never caught me again.

My father had a weekend business trip a few years later so once I knew for a fact he was states away, I rushed back into my sisters' room. I put on a dress and a pair of heels, but when I went to look in the mirror to put on my makeup, I froze. I stared at my reflection and the only thing I could think about was the look in my father's eyes when he caught me. I felt disgusted. I knew in my heart what I was doing was making me happy, but questioned if it was really worth making my father sad. I was the son he waited years to have, the miracle boy. I knew there was one thing I could do that would end the suffering for both of us.

I put my sisters' things back and went into my room. In my closet I had tucked away the hunting knife that my grandfather gave me for my birthday one year. I hated hunting but my grandfather loved it. I took the knife out and unzipped my pants. If I couldn't be the man my father wanted to raise, then I didn't deserve to be a man at all. I had no idea how to rewire my brain to like girls, so I thought I would reconstruct my body to become something that would be accepted for liking boys.

I made one cut into my penis and then another that was a little deeper than the first. When the pain became unbearable, I threw the knife back into the closet. I cried on the floor with my pants to my ankles for what seemed like hours, eventually crying myself to sleep. When I woke up I pulled my pants up and went to ask my mom for pain killers. I told her it was because I had a headache. She gave me the pills and I went back into my room. I took about five pills before passing out on my bed.

I continued to struggle with my desires. Every time I pictured myself happy with a man, I pictured my father in a casket and I wanted to cut all over again. If I were to die, all of the suffering would end. The desires wouldn't exist if I were dead and my father's pain wouldn't exist. I couldn't take it anymore; I was going to do it again. I was going to try to kill myself again, but this time I wouldn't leave any room for error.

I picked a random school day to pretend to be sick. My mother said I could stay home and get better. When my sisters left for school and my parents left for work I was alone. I waited for about two hours to make sure no one would pop up, then I made my move. I climbed out of my bed, cleaned up my room and placed my suicide letter on top of my pillow. Then I went to the garage and grabbed a piece of rope that I had cut and tied into a noose earlier that week. We had this huge oak tree in the backyard that I would sit under whenever I needed to clear my head; the air just seemed cleaner. Because it was my place for comfort in life, I concluded that it would be my place for comfort in the afterlife as well. Using a ladder, I climbed to the first branch and tied the rope around it before putting the other end, that was already looped, around my neck. I stood on the ladder and stared into my neighborhood; it was perfect. All of the lawns were cut and there was no trash in site. The morning newspapers sat on each doorstep and the birds flew in the air, chirping pure joy. Everything and everyone was perfect…except for me. It would be selfish of me to continue to be the thing that ruins the neighborhood and I knew it was time. I stepped off of the ladder.

I'm not sure what I was expecting to feel after I stepped off the ladder, but I knew what I was feeling was not right. I questioned if I would automatically feel cold or instantly be able to feel nothing at all, but instead I felt arms on my legs. Apparently as I was staring off into my neighborhood, one of my neighbors was staring at me. The trance that I was in made it impossible to notice that someone was running into my yard and up the ladder; when I stepped off to what I believed to be the end, I was actually stepping into her arms.

"I am not letting you do this Craig!" It was my neighbor from across the street, Amanda. The combination of sincerity and sadness in her voice was a sound I'd never heard before. It was then, that I knew what love was.

Still holding onto my body, Amanda climbed to the top of the ladder and cut me down. Reluctantly, I walked down the ladder with her, as I contemplated on how I would try again when I knew for sure no one else was around. I needed a funeral more than I needed a hero.

When we were both down, we just sat in the grass; it was awkward to say the least. She turned to me with tears still streaming down her face and quietly asked,

"Why?"

In my head, the plan was to ignore her until she left me alone, but my heart couldn't take anymore silence. I released a wail, crying like a baby as I told her everything. From me being gay, to my other suicide attempts, to my father catching me. I told it all. Things fell silent. She wasn't saying anything, the birds were no longer chirping, and I knew I had just made a huge mistake. I started to get up and go inside but she grabbed my arm, pulled me back down, and hugged me. The tears began to fall all over again.

"It is ok to love whoever your heart desires Craig. Nothing is wrong with you, nothing at all and I love you for the man you are."

Her hug magically sealed together all of my broken pieces; for the first time in years I felt whole.

Amanda didn't want me to hide who I was anymore, but she also didn't want my father to kick me out, so she devised a plan. She was going to play my girlfriend so my father would believe that being gay was just a phase. Once he thought I was straight, he would love me again. He would have to love me again.

I graduated high school without ever dressing in women's clothes again or attempting suicide. As a graduation gift, my parents agreed to let me have a party in the house. It was a full house and we had gotten enough kegs, that no cup went empty. I've always been a light -weight when it came to drinking, but it was a celebration and it was quite possible that I had one too many. The fear kept me quiet about who I really was and the desire to have Amanda pretend to be my girlfriend, all disappeared. That night I was in the mood to just be me.

The party was going on downstairs in the basement but I just wanted a moment to breathe, so I went upstairs. When I went upstairs I saw Tony. Tony had been my neighbor for about eight years and secretly my crush for most of that time. He played tennis and was on the swim team and he had a body sculpted by God and GQ. I took another sip of my beer for liquid courage and walked up to him.

"What's up Craig?"

My name leaving his lips made my penis do a backflip. I knew it was now or never. I told him, "This is what's up Tony," and I kissed him. I just kissed him. At that very moment, my father walked in. It is like he has a gaydar. My parents had agreed to stay away for the night, but my father had to come back to get his briefcase; he was known for his horrible timing. The rest of the night happened so fast.

My father screamed "Get the fuck out of my house you fucking faggot!" Tony pushed me away and pulled his hand back to punch me. At the last minute, he just walked out of the house. I grabbed my wallet, my phone, my jacket and ran out. That was the last time I talked to my father.

After about a week of living in a hotel, I decided to reach out to my mother and sisters. My mother didn't even bother to return my calls or texts. I couldn't say that I was surprised; she loved him more than she loved me. She loved everyone more than she loved me. My sisters, on the other hand, wanted to help. They were all in college in different states, but they booked me a bus ticket and I made my way to their campuses. For two months everything worked out fine. They let me use their meal plans and sleep on their couches, I had even started making friends everywhere...but then I got caught.

I was sneaking into Collie's room, the second oldest, and a security guard caught me. She lived in an all-female dorm so brother or not, I was not allowed to be there after hours. The guard ended up calling my father and telling him that he had caught a boy sneaking into my sister's room. She, of course, told him that it was just me; thinking that he would be relieved. I think he would have rather had some guy sticking his dick into his daughter. My father was far from dumb and he knew that if she was doing it, then my other sisters probably were too. He gave them an ultimatum; they could either let me stay and lose his financial support or kick me out. It was either stay in college or help their little gay, disgusting fairy of a brother. I loved my sisters too much to make them decide, so I decided for them. I left.

I lived under a bridge for two and a half years and was working as a mascot for a children's restaurant. I was only making enough money to eat and stay at hotels periodically. I had no idea how I was to afford much more making minimum wage. I had almost accepted that this would be my life, until I heard some people talking about this center and how Ms. Green was such a kind spirited person to be around and that she truly cared about people like me. I hitched a ride and made my way here. Honey, it was the best decision I made for myself in a very long time.

Chapter Six - Part Two

I experimented with my sexuality in college, but never joined the league. I cannot begin to imagine what my parents would have done if I told them that I was gay or even admitted that I had sex with a woman or two. If I ever met a woman with a healthy bank account and willing to give me full access, I would consider it though. If love doesn't have a gender, why should power?

"Craig, have you talked to you sisters since you've been here?"

"We speak when we can. Only in secrecy."

Francesca giggled. "Every man has a secret. I had my suspicions you were a butt pirate but didn't want to assume."

"Oh well thank you Frannie. You're such a kind woman."

"I know. It's a tough job but someone has to do it to counteract Tori's cold shoulder."

Tori smirked. "We all have our roles to play."

Apparently, Tori's role was to always get her two cents in.

"Craig, so you are telling me that you could not just be straight or keep it in your pants long enough to make sure your dad did not kick you out? Did everyone in here just want to be homeless?"

"Pause, let me stop you right there doc. I did not choose to be gay any more than you chose to be straight. There have been many a night when I kneeled in the gravel under that bridge until my knees bled, praying that God would just make me straight. Everything would be ok if he could just make me normal. You think I wouldn't have rather been in college, like my sisters, following my dreams and still have a loving place to call home. I would give my hearing, if the last words I heard could be I love you by my father. After my parents had me, my mother got her tubes tied because the family they wanted was finally complete. There was finally a boy that would one day grow to be a man that could continue their legacy. I just happened to be gay. I just had to come out broken. I have called on every higher power begging, pleading, and bargaining to just be made straight. I have even had sex with a few women hoping that being gay was just a feeling, just a phase, just a craving that would one day subside. I knew what I was feeling and what I was doing was wrong, but I couldn't help it. So you can criticize me for what I wear or who my friends are because those are my choices. I was born gay and I chose to live in my truth. Don't you dare have the audacity to stand in your glass house and tell me that I chose this homeless lifestyle. No one chooses this lifestyle."

I began clapping my hands. "That was a cute little speech, but my opinion still remains the same. People live lives they do not enjoy all of the time and it works. You could have simply married a woman, had a few kids, and lived a life that your father would not be ashamed of. You knew the consequences for being gay and you still decided not to change. I would probably rather see my child dead, than gay."

"My father thought the same thing and trust me sweetheart I have tried that too. I guess I'm just too gay to slice my wrists straight."

The sound that followed almost caused me to jump out of my perfectly tanned skin. Tori had gotten up and knocked her chair to the floor.

"You are a bitch. I was really trying to be respectful to you because I assumed somewhere under your diamonds and tailored suits there was a human being, but I was wrong. Here we are pouring our hearts out to you, sharing our wounds and you are judging us. That's not being helpful; that's being a spoiled little rich bitch. People like you are the reason..."

"Excuse me! Ms. Tori you have yet to open your mouth unless sarcasm is spurring out. If you are so focused, so concerned about how I am reacting to everyone else's story, then how about you tell me yours?"

"You don't deserve to hear my story or anyone else's in this group. You better get ready doc because you just made the next 358 days of your life a living hell. I suggest you bring a book or two tomorrow because it's lonely in your own thoughts. We can't make you sit in here alone because it is a condition of us staying here that we come to these sessions, but we can make it lonely. Our eyes are going to be the sources to your nightmares soon enough, mark my words."

Chapter Seven

I debated on not going in today after Tori's little outburst, but under the conditions of my punishment, I was not allowed to miss a day unless I had an excuse. I am thirty-two years old and I had been reduced to having to ask my doctor for a sick note so I would not go to jail. Just a year; I just have to get through a year of this and then I was off to enjoy the rest of my life and leave this horrid memory in the past.

Lily was not at the front desk this morning. It was a bit of a relief. I knew someone from group would have told her what happened and I was just not in the mood to hear one of her holier than thou speeches today. I wanted to go into the room, conduct my session and get the hell out of here. Today is my wedding anniversary and I knew Sebastian would want me home to celebrate as soon as possible. That man simply adores me.

"Hello everyone. How are you all feeling today?"No one said anything. The room was so quiet you could hear an old man tell his young wife no.

"I asked how you all are feeling today. Am I not talking loud enough or do you all have old Chinese food in your ears from the dumpster diving last night?"

The room remained silent."Are you all really going to play this game? I would ask where your manners were but I am sure they were abandoned somewhere along with your self-esteem or work ethic."

They all just continued to do whatever it was they were doing before I walked into the room. It was like I was not even there.

"Well the joke is on you all because I would much rather sit here and do something productive with my life, like balance my checkbook than listen to grown people blame everything and everybody for their problems."

Time moved like someone had jammed it into a jar of molasses, and then turned the jar on its side. This had to have been the longest day in my life and when time was up I could not get out of that building quick enough. The good news was I could go home and tell my husband all about it while he washed my feet.

Chapter Eight

"Honey I am home, Happy Anniversary baby! You would not believe what these people did today."

My voice echoed in the house. It was empty. "Honey? Sebastian?"

I went into the garage to see if his car was there but it was not. He must have had to work for a little while today. I know he is still playing catch up from not having Tony at work but he better not let that keep him from coming home soon. After all, it is our anniversary.

I could hear every tick as it passed the previous sixty seconds. Every minute that passed grabbed a piece of my hope on its way out. I decided I would just keep myself busy until he came home. It was too late to go out for dinner so he would probably bring food home and we could cuddle up with dinner and a movie, simple but sweet. Well if I was to be cuddle worthy, I should probably soak off the filth of the shelter today.

I went upstairs and ran a hot bath. I completed the full scene with soft music and bubbles. My body was actually pretty sore today and since Sebastian was not here to put some pressure on my back, I was left to do it myself. Thankfully, I have a bath jet. I start on my back, but my hand slipped and the jet fell into the water. At first I was frightened, but then I remembered the jet was waterproof. My initial fear was soon replaced with another emotion.

Between Sebastian working to expand the company, me going through the whole court situation, and then working at the shelter, we have not had a lot of us time lately. When the jet hit the water, it was still vibrating. There was another place that needed some attention, a place that needed some attention badly. Very badly.

I lifted my right leg out of the water onto the edge of the bath and allowed the rest of my body to emerge. Armed with the jet in my hand, I found my vagina. It felt sinful and that excited me even more. I put the jet right on top of my clitoris. Oh, fuck. I bit down on my lip hard enough to rip it off, but it felt so good. I allowed two of my fingers to find their way into my vagina with the jet still in place. I started off slowly teasing my orgasm, soaking in every moment of pleasure. When I could not hold off any longer, I sped up, slipping my now three fingers, in and out, in and out of my vagina. I dropped the jet into the water and used my other hand to grope my breast, lifting them to my mouth and massaging my nipples with my tongue. Oh, my God! Oh, shit, fuck, I'm I'm… My moans filled the bathroom and for that one moment I was elated that Sebastian was not home yet. He has never made me react that way.

I must have done a better job than I thought because I woke up in a tub of ice cold water. What time was it? I got out of the tub, grabbed my robe and went into the bedroom. Sebastian was not in the bed. I checked the alarm clock for the time; it was one in the morning. I checked my phone for any missed notifications, but I did not have any. Where in the hell was Sebastian?

I walked downstairs and found my answer. Sebastian was on the couch, knocked out with his computer on his lap and his phone still in his hand. Beside him on the couch covered in papers and a calculator was Tony. Sebastian was so determined to be home for our anniversary that he dragged poor Tony home with him. It was so sweet.

I went to the couch to clean up and get these hard working men to a more comfortable place to sleep. I tried to be as quiet as possible not to wake them. I grabbed Sebastian's phone out of his hand and lifted his computer from his lap. Without the laptop in the way I could see that his pants were unbuttoned and his zipper was down. I pushed the papers off of Tony and saw that his penis was out of his pants with the condom still on.

"Are you fucking serious?" Sebastian and Tony both jump up and stared at me like deers in my headlight.

"Tony get up, put your penis away, and get the hell out of my house!"

"Mrs. Thomas I'm so sorry."

"Out!"

Tony ran out of the house with his shoes in hand, still trying to zip his pants up.

"Good morning to you too Taylor."

Sebastian made a half-ass attempt to zip and button his pants. "Sebastian do not good morning me right now. Do you even know what yesterday was?"

"Wednesday, I believe."

"That is right. It was Wednesday the eleventh, our anniversary."

"Ok? I'm still not seeing your point. Why would we celebrate an arrangement?"

"Because that is what married couples do Sebastian! One thing they do not do is bring their boyfriend home and screw him with their wife upstairs."

"Look, you knew I was gay when you agreed to marry me. You wanted to be rich and I wanted a beautiful wife to show off to my business partners, we both won."

"I never agreed for you to treat me like I wasn't a real person or to screw your assistant in our house! You want to get rammed in the ass that is fine, find another place to do it."

"So, what are you going to do now Tay? Are you going to leave me, leave my money? Everything you have…everything you will ever have comes out of my pocket! Now, if you are done with your little tantrum, I would like to shower. Oh…and if you are ready to be a stay at home mom, therefore fulfilling the rest of the terms of the agreement, then I will leave this here."

Sebastian took off the condom that he had used last night and put it on the table.

"No matter what agreement we have I still deserve the right to be treated like a human with emotions!"

"Why? You've never treated me like a human. I was always just a piggy bank with a dick. And what about the humans at the shelter huh? Look at how you treat them, how you talk about them. Do you really believe that anyone that knows you thinks you are human? No! You're just a vain, heartless, egotistical narcissist. You aren't capable of emotions. I'm going to do what I want, so just sit back, shut up and enjoy the lifestyle."

I wanted to cry but he was right. I knew that Sebastian was just looking to get married as a cover and I said yes. He gave me my perfect wedding with all of our family and friends gathered around to witness it. Everyone said I had never looked happier. What they did not see was that we spent our honeymoon in separate rooms. We booked the honeymoon suite but when we were on the beach having dinner Sebastian was lusting for our waiter. He came in later that night and told me that he had booked another room for the two of them but insisted that I order anything that I wanted from room service. That night I ordered two of everything and five bottles of champagne. Most of it was wasted but it made me feel better to rack up a three-thousand-dollar room service bill for Sebastian to pay for.

I got dressed, grabbed my purse, and left. It was definitely time to shop.

Chapter Nine

Between the tension at home on the rise and still getting the silent treatment from the group at the shelter, I was losing my mind. “Good morning Lily.”

“Good morning Dr. Thomas.”

“Lily I just want to thank you.”

“Thank me for what?”

“For not giving me the silent treatment like everyone else here. I know I am a bitch most of the time, but the silence is killing me.”

“In the last few days you’ve shown me something I never expected from you and I’m just wondering what happened.”

“What did I show you?”

“That you are human, that you could allow your Botox to relax long enough to frown.”

“Well a few days ago something happened that made me feel again. It made me realize that I could still hurt. Things could happen in my life and when I looked around I had no one to share them.”

“What about your husband?”

“What about my husband?”

"Hmm… moving on. Well if you want them to start back opening up to you, then you have to show them that emotion. You've never shown them that you're human."

"You might be right."

"No harm in trying."

That was exactly what I was going to do. I would walk into that room and I would try. I had to do something, because I was still a long ways away from a year and I would go crazy attempting to continue it like this.

"Hello everyone."

Silence.

"So, it looks like you all are going to do a year of the silent treatment? Good to know."

Silence.

"Well I have good news for you guys. I am not interested in talking to you all today. No, I am much more interested in you all listening to what I have to say. My name is Taylor Thomas. Dr. Taylor Thomas. In my thirty-two years of living I have never had to work or fear that I could not have any and everything that I wanted. First, it was my father and now, it's my husband taking care of me. We have the perfect relationship… from the outside. In reality, I only married him to maintain the lifestyle I am accustomed. He gives me whatever I want so I can smile for the cameras and be his pretty wife. He needed a pretty wife because no one wants to do business with a gay man. Gay men do not go to spousal holiday parties or family barbeques. So, see Frannie you called it… every man has a secret."

While waiting for someone else to say something after I revealed my secret, I began to think. What if all of this was a mistake and they did not care about anything that was going on in my life. I should never have listened to a wannabe doctor working in a shit hole for the hell of it. I should just have brought in more books and did my time in silence. I would just bring in my tablet tomorrow and do some online shopping while they sit there and twirl their thumbs, recalling the many mistakes that had led them to their miserable excuses of life. I should have just…

"I'm James."

It was a new voice, unfamiliar, yet comforting. After only listening to the pipes leak for the last few days, any form of person to person communication was comforting.

"Nice to meet you James. How are you feeling today?"

"Normal. Well it's normal for me, crazy for the rest of the world."

"Why would your normal be crazy for the rest of the world?"

"Because that is what I am doc and that is how I got here. I am crazy."

JAMES

Just do it, kill yourself. No one will be upset that a bottom feeder is dead. They might actually give you a soldier's burial for doing the world a favor. You are worthless and don't even deserve the dirt floor your mother probably had you on. Why do you think she left you? She left you to kill herself because she knew you wouldn't accomplish anything in life. She didn't want to just sit around waiting for the inevitable.

These were just some of the things the voices used to tell me daily. When I was growing up they weren't as evil; they would tell me to steal a cookie before dinner or trip a kid that was picking on me. Nothing really bad. It seemed like the older I got, the worse the voices got. I could handle them, but when I started seeing things, I learned later on weren't really there, I knew it was time to tell someone.

It went on for years before I told someone. I found myself having full conversations with the voices. I would plead and bargain for them to just leave me alone. I constantly questioned them as to why they chose me. WHY ME?!? At one point, I concluded I was Jesus, God's Son, sent to Earth to carry out his orders. Why else could I hear and see things no one else could? There was no other explanation. My grandmother would tell me of the miracles that God performed and the stories almost read as memories; like I physically watched as my father defied reality. 'Trust in the Lord with all your heart and lean not on your own understanding; in all your ways acknowledge him and he will make your paths straight'. Proverbs 3:5-6. My grandmother embedded the Bible into my brain with the intention of helping me remember who I was. When the voices became dangerous, I knew I was not Jesus. The things they were saying, the things I was seeing… there was nothing Holy about them.

I turned to the person that raised me, my grandmother. I was about three when she took me in and I couldn't have been more thankful for it. Foster care was my next option had she not agreed to take me. Both my parents were dead, murder/suicide. The story goes that my mother found out my dad was touching me in ways he wasn't supposed to. My grandmother told me that my mother had her suspicions, so she hooked up a nanny cam in my bedroom. They watched the video together, well, started watching it... They saw my dad get naked in my room and put his hand in my shorts; that was more than enough evidence for my mother. When my grandmother first told me the story, years after I had moved in with her, I felt paralyzed. How could I not have known he was doing something wrong to me. He told me it was a way of showing love and I believed him.

The last thing my grandmother said she heard my mother say was "I'm going to kill him!" She called my grandmother and asked her to take care of me because she knew that night would not end well for anyone. I can at least say my mother was a woman of her word.

She killed him and after she realized what she had done, she turned the gun onto herself. I was in my room when it all happened. The first gunshot literally scared the piss out of me. I froze. I did not move from my bed until a police officer came in. Honestly… I think my mother heard the voices too. No one ever told me that she did, but by some of the stories they told me about her, I kind of just knew.

I was ten when I admitted to my grandmother that I was seeing things that I knew for a fact weren't there and hearing voices inside of my head. I would see thousands of ants come out of the vents and attack her, or the floor would suddenly be covered with snakes. I would have to shake my head or beat on my head for the images to go away. I would use water bottles, books, anything I could get my hands on to beat my head until they shut up or I passed out from the blows. My grandmother told me things had gotten worse because I turned my back on God. She was disappointed that I had steered so far away from the way she raised me.

From that point on I made it my mission to live a good, clean Christian lifestyle. I hated the idea that I had disappointed the only person that agreed to take me in. I didn't have sex or drink. I would even ask for forgiveness after I said a curse word. Would you believe that even after praying every single night, promising that if he would just clear my mind of the voices, I would continue to be perfect…nothing changed. It seemed like the harder I prayed, the stronger the voices became. They were not fans of hope.

I went to my grandmother again and told her that my prayers were going unheard and I could still hear the voices. She said to me, "Baby you ain't praying right. If you want him to hear you then you gotta go to his house, you gotta go to church." I told her that I would go with her the following week but before I made it to church that Sunday to pray, my grandmother died. I couldn't go to church without her; I didn't know what to say. I had already wasted so much time praying the wrong way. I needed her to tell me how to pray the correct way so that I could get rid of the voices once and for all.

It was then that I knew God had it in for me. First, he stole my parents from me, then he cursed me with voices and hallucinations and now he took the only person on Earth willing to help me get better. I would constantly question what I must have done for him to punish me this way. I pinpointed my grandmother's death as the beginning to the end for me.

When my grandmother died none of my other family members wanted to take care of me. The rest of my family knew my mother heard voices and even though I never told them, they figured I was just like her. They quickly refused to take me in. I simply took this act as another form of punishment being enforced upon me by the Almighty. I became numb to bad news after my grandmother died. My grandmother was my first example of real love. I knew it was love because the heartbreak from losing her felt permanent.

Due to no relatives stepping forward I was sent to a group home. The walls were cold and rained blood. The thick blood would sink into the bricks, completely transforming them. In my room, I could hear the cries of the children that lived there before me. "Get out of my bed!" "I'm going to kill you!" "There's no way out!"

My first thought was to tell the counselor what was going on, but then I remembered what happened when I told my grandmother. She tried to help me and God killed her for it. I fully understood the consequences of speaking out against the voices. They were stronger than me, smarter than me and they would always win. There was no helping me, I was alone in this world. I refused to be the cause of another death because they tried to help me. I had to find a way to help myself.

One day, as I was walking back to the group home after school, I stopped and bought a gun in an alley where they didn't allow prayer. The voices were quiet during the entire time, so I knew I had finally found something that scared them. I also knew they would send children that stayed in the room before me to attack me and steal my gun. I snuck the gun in my coat and put it under my pillow. When it was time for lights out, the voices and hallucinations started like clockwork. I could hear them in the kitchen going through the drawers and grabbing weapons. Tonight was the night. Tonight they were coming to kill me.

The night was still for hours; my eyes were becoming heavier and heavier as the clock ticked. Maybe I was wrong about it being tonight. As I replaced the gun and laid down, I heard them. My heart raced as their footsteps got louder and louder…they were almost at the door. I heard someone jiggle the lock. I knew that I had to stop them before they got through the door. I grabbed the gun from under my pillow and squeezed the trigger three times.

Bang! Bang! Bang!

… the voices were gone; the entire room fell silent.

I got up out of my bed and ran to open the door. I beat the voices! I could be normal for the first time in my life!! I didn't see anyone. I stepped out to see if I missed and they had run down the hall. I felt something wet and thick on my feet; it reminded me of almost ready jello. I looked down.

The sight of blood must have snapped me back into reality because I realized the person at the door wasn't some stranger from my head, it was one of the kids that lived in the home. He was about four years old. This was by far the worst punishment placed on me. I had become the very monstert my family assumed I would be. I had killed an innocent child and there was nothing that I could do to bring him back. I slumped down to his body and pulled him up into my lap.

The gun shots had awakened the counselor and she came sprinting down the hallway. She couldn't believe what she saw; I didn't want to believe what I had done. I sat on the floor rocking back and forth singing gospel songs as the counselor called the police. When the cops arrived, they arrested me. As they led me out of the home and into the police car, the voices started back… they were mocking me. "You missed stupid idiot." "We were right there and instead you murdered a child that had done nothing to you." "Ha! ha! ha!, you're even worse than us. We just talk the talk, but you." "Oh, you walk the walk."

The whole booking process is fuzzy to me. I would close my eyes and see the little boy dead in my arms. Eventually, I just stopped closing them. I knew I was in trouble, but when they questioned me of my motives I couldn't even defend myself. What was I going to say, that the voices made me do it? No one would believe that. Everyone would just call me crazy and my crazy ass would spend the rest of my life in jail.

My counselor called the group's lawyer and he was able to prove that I was not guilty due to mental disease or deficit. Mental disease was just a fancy word for crazy. They knew something was wrong with me, they knew I was cursed, and they knew there was nothing that could help me. The judge sentenced me to a mental hospital until I was eighteen.

The next eight years were easy in comparison to life before that. The only downside was the constant experiments with medication. They were determined to find a combination that made me sane, while keeping me lucid. The pines, the zines, the zoles, and dones…I have tried them all. I have ingested and injected enough drugs to sing lead for a boy group. For the first few months, they had to forcefully give them to me, but when I noticed that my thoughts were quiet and my vision was clear, I started to take them willingly. On my eighteenth birthday, I was released from the hospital and with a newly expunged record I set out to succeed in life. I was a free man; the voices were gone, and I had the freedom to hope for more.

When I left the hospital, they gave me a packet of information and $50. What now? They didn't really give me a direction when I left, but even worse than that, they didn't prepare me for life without the medication they consistently gave me. They don't tell you when they are giving you the pills that when they wear off the voices would come rushing back with a vengeance. It's like they are mad at you for taking the pills to make them go away, so they make you pay for it by telling you to do deadly things. "Kill yourself." "It's time to pull the trigger." "Don't be a punk." "Do the world a favor."

I wanted the voices to go away again but the medication I was given in the mental hospital was so expensive. I was eighteen with no job and no high school diploma; there was no way I could afford them. I concluded that I would have to find my own medication. As it turns out, I could drown the voices in gin. I was up to drinking half a gallon of gin a day and with the odd jobs I picked up, I could afford my new medicine.

All I did was drink and sleep, sleep and drink. You would assume I had an abundance of energy due to the amount of sleep I had every day, but it was the exact opposite. I would go to sleep exhausted and wake up the same way; no amount of time was enough. I would become furious with myself. Like, how could I not function without feeling like I weighed a thousand pounds.

By the time I was twenty-five, I was selling drugs to support my habit. Friends would tell me the coke I was selling would help my voices stay away better than the alcohol, but I couldn't break the main rule of the business: don't get high on your own supply. Plus, why fix a system that wasn't broken. As long as I was sloshed the voices were silent.

Between my drinking and my business, I lived on the party scene. Different night, different city. People would probably have said that I was quite popular, but in reality, I could not have felt any more alone. All the people started running in together. I didn't see them as individuals; I barely saw them as humans. They were merely pawns in my grand scheme of life. One of the men that I started selling drugs with was gunned down right in front of me during a drug deal gone wrong and I was just happy that it wasn't me. I gave his mom five thousand dollars for the funeral and moved on to the next city.

In every new group of people that I submerged myself, I could feel they knew something was wrong with me. I would do the best I could to mask my depression, but some aspects would peek through and make them question. Strangely enough, the feeling made me envious of those with physical, or even evident, mental disabilities. When you see someone in a wheelchair you automatically know they can't walk. You might not know what went wrong, but you know what *is* wrong. Even when you see someone with Downs Syndrome, you can tell that something is wrong. The disability might be mental, but the way it showed up physically made you aware of what was wrong. My disability, my disease… it was all in my head. No one else could hear the voices or see the dogs rip off the faces of children, so no one could tell what was wrong with me. On the outside, I looked normal, so everyone assumed I was also normal on the inside. I was sick and the worst part about it was everyone knew but no one could help me. I could tell this punishment would follow me the rest of my life.

My body eventually became immune to the alcohol, because when I was about twenty-seven, it stopped working. Things weren't perfect, but they were going well enough for me to function, and just like that…normality was ripped away from me. The voices came back, and this time, their anger was too strong to ignore. I was walking to the store one day when I heard them say, "it's time, kill yourself now or we will send someone to do it for you. No one is going to miss you when you are gone, no one loves you. No one will ever love you. End it! End it now!"

I couldn't fight them anymore… maybe I just didn't want to fight them anymore. The only way to permanently get rid of the voices was to permanently get rid of myself. Plus, they were right. The life I was living was worthless and no one would miss me when I was gone. No one would ever love me. How could anyone possibly love me? …I was crazy.

I ran out of the store and into the middle of the road during rush hour traffic. A taxi caught me on my left side and launched me thirty feet. I assumed I passed out as soon as my body hit the concrete because when I came to, I was in the hospital, handcuffed to the bed. My leg was in a cast, but other than that, I was only covered in scratches and bruises. God clearly wanted my punishment to last longer, so he made it impossible for me to even commit suicide.

The doctor placed me on a 72 hour suicide watch. He came in and I told him that I had previously been in a mental hospital and asked if I could get the same medications because they worked. He asked me what I was diagnosed with and shamefully I could not tell him. I never thought there were different names for crazy. He asked me, what felt like a hundred questions, and told me that he would run a few tests to confirm his diagnosis.

"Schizophrenia." It was the first time I heard it out loud. My type of crazy was schizophrenia. The voices, the hallucinations, and the lack of everything; it all told him that I had schizophrenia. He started me on the combination of meds and they worked perfectly. What didn't work out perfectly, was trying to get a job with a diagnosis of crazy. I might as well had tattooed it onto my forehead.

Currently, I am making enough money here and there to afford my medications and food. There are times when I want to go back to my lifestyle of selling drugs because it made a lot more money, but I knew what came with it. I knew the world I was once in was not healthy, and it would drag me back to Hell. The medications are way more expensive than the alcohol, but they would also kill me a lot slower than gin.

Chapter Nine - Part Two

James looked far from crazy, he looked more like, drive them crazy. He had beautiful, clear skin, broad shoulders, washboard abs, and a perfect smile. He had just enough facial hair to look like a grown man, but not too much where he looked like a Neanderthal.

"I knew there had to be something wrong with a man as fine as you are to be in a place like this."

"I guess I'll take that as a compliment Tori."

"Take it however you want James, whatever helps you sleep at night."

I was just happy the silence was gone. Looks like Lily was right about me just opening up to them. I had to wonder if it would have a domino effect on the rest of the group.

"So, you envy people like me? That's new."

The question came from the corner of the room, a voice I hadn't heard before.

"Yes, I do Lauren and I know it's weird. I guess that just adds to the whole, I'm crazy thing."

Lauren had to have been the youngest one in the group, no older than seventeen; but just by looking at her you knew she had a story beyond her years. She was pretty and well-kept for a homeless kid, and was also in a wheelchair. Like James said, we might not know how she got there, but it was obvious that something was wrong. She reminded me of someone; I just could not place who. On another note, I could not help but wonder where her parents were and how they could let their teenage daughter roam the streets alone in a wheelchair.

"So technically you're like a hardened criminal?"

There was another new voice. She looked like one of the younger girls in the group, but still older than Lauren. I could not remember her name, but she was a redhead. Her hair was curly and her eyes were exotic. She was in a sweatsuit that was clearly too big for her and her sneakers looked like the prison had issued them and *massa* made her break them in on the field.

"I wouldn't refer to myself as hardened, Naomi. I was only in jail for a few days before I was transferred to the mental hospital. I killed a little boy, and not a day goes by that I don't see his face, or wonder where he could have been in life, if I hadn't pulled that trigger."

Naomi. Her name is Naomi, got it.

"No, it's cool, I'm not judging. I've been in before myself."

"You? Now what would a pretty little thing like you be doing to go to a place like that? I'm sure that you could have talked and batted your eyelashes out of any situation."

"You're right, I could have."

"Then, why didn't you?"

"I wanted to go to jail."

"Ok, now you have got to spill. It was already weird that doc thought that we all wanted to be homeless, but for someone wanting to go to jail, that's downright insane."

I didn't know James was even listening when I was talking in the beginning. Was I really that bad? Maybe Sebastian was right. Actually, there is no maybe, he was right. I am doing better now because I'm actually engaged with them. I can continue to do better; I can learn how to be…human.

"Why would you want to go to jail, Naomi?"

"Dr. Thomas, jail gave me everything that I couldn't give myself."

"Like what?"

"Food, shelter, a bed; it all came free and easy in jail."

"But you were not free."

"My freedom was the price I was willing to pay. I was just wasting it living on the streets anyway."

NAOMI

My story doesn't have all the glitz and glamour that most of yours do. I was born and sold to the streets. You know how most expectant mothers are excited to be bringing another human into the world? Yeah, well, that wasn't my mother. My mother could not wait to get me out so she could put my existence in her rearview mirror.

My mother was seventeen when she came to the states in hopes of a better life. America: home of the free, land of the dreamers. She started working at a local diner and was saving money to start taking night classes. The night classes were the easiest part for her.

My mother was a natural scholar. Anything academic came easy to her. After only taking classes for a few months, she was already a year ahead of schedule and wanted to add another major. Another major would mean more classes and more classes would mean more money. She decided to pick up late night shifts at the diner. She would work in the morning, go to class, then work another shift when she got out of class. My mother was determined to have everything that the American lifestyle had to offer.

One night, as she was closing the diner with her boss, he made her a proposition. If she would have sex with him, he would give her a raise and pay her rent for a month. He knew she was spending most of her money on classes and needed any extra money she could get. He also knew she was an immigrant and not privy to certain assistance programs. My mother said no.

Every night after that he would ask and every night she would say no.

This went on for months. Her boss grew colder every time she turned him down, until his heart had completely frozen solid. As my mother was in the back cleaning up one night, her boss was in the front locking all of the doors and pulling down the blinds. My mother came out and headed for the door and her boss was right behind her. She knew he would ask the same question he had been asking for months, so before he could, she turned to him and said, “No thank you.” In a soulless voice, he replied, “I’m not asking.”

With that said, he grabbed my mother by her throat, and dragged her to the back. She was a feisty one; she kicked his legs and scratched at his hands but he was too strong. When they made it to the hallway, he let go of her throat and pushed her down to the floor. He looked at the scratches she had made on his hands, laughed and licked the blood away before getting on top of her and kissing her on the mouth. My mother begged and pleaded that he stop, nothing worked. Her boss yanked off her pants and told her if she tried to get up, he would kill her. Fearing for her life, she laid on the floor stunned, trying to picture herself anywhere but there. In her mind, she was in her bed and this was merely a nightmare. The horrible reality was that she was on a cold floor being raped.

What a sick, ironic, twist because once he was done and she knew what happened, the real horror began. My mother never went back to that diner or any diner in fact. She couldn’t focus on her classes and ended up flunking out of all of them. Now she had no job, no money, and no degree.

For months, she pushed it back deeper and deeper into her memory. She had pushed it so deep that she could almost forget that it happened. She was almost ready to start over when she went to the doctor and found out something that made everything come rushing back. She was pregnant.

My mother was a virgin when her boss raped her and lived in fear that any guy she got close to would hurt her, so she didn't get close to any of them. My mother was pregnant and she knew it could only mean one thing. The man that raped her left a piece of him behind and now she had a rapist's baby growing inside of her. How could she ever love something that was conceived in fear and pain? The very idea of carrying me sent her into a deep depression. The very hole she was climbing out of was now pulling her back in, and someone was throwing dirt on top to make sure she never got out again.

She made up her mind that she would get an abortion, but they didn't come free. My mother had already lost everything, including her hope, so she did the only thing she thought that she could. To come up with the money for an abortion, she started stealing from stores and selling the things on the streets. Purses, clothes, shoes; it didn't matter. If it was not nailed to the ground and it was worth something she would try to steal it. There was a huge risk in stealing and selling stolen goods, but every outcome from it was positive to her. If she stole and sold, she would make enough money for the abortion. If she got caught and went to jail, they would take me as soon as I popped out anyway. And if someone found out what she was doing and killed her, at least she wouldn't have to carry her unwanted child anymore. No matter what happened she was going to win and I was going to lose. Before I was even able to take my first breath, it had been decided that I was going to lose.

Unfortunately for my mother, she never got the chance to have an abortion. She was trying to save the money, but time didn't stop just because of that. She was about seven months pregnant before she saved up enough money; too far along for any ethical doctor to perform the surgery. No one ever caught her stealing so she didn't go to jail and no one wanted to retaliate and kill her, so she was stuck. Stuck carrying a baby that she wanted nothing more than to get rid of and forget ever existed. She even tried alternative ways to kill me, but the drinking made her sick, and launching herself down a flight of stairs just left her with bruises.

On October $19^{th,}$ she gave birth to me. My mother told me that she was just going to leave me at the hospital the first chance she got, but her plans changed when the doctor placed me in her arms. She looked down at me and saw that I had her eyes… at that very moment she realized that I was her child too. I guess she could only focus on me being a rapist's baby while I was growing inside of her, but for the first time she saw that I was her baby too; that I had lived and grown in her stomach for nine months. She told me that was the day she fell in love for the first time.

Having a kid did not help getting off of the streets. She moved up from stealing from stores to stealing a lot of folks' credit card information. Identity thief was a much more serious charge and when she got caught she landed in jail for it. With no one to take care of me, I ended up in a jail of my own, foster care. I bounced around to eleven different foster homes until they kicked me out when I turned eighteen. They were making sure that I went to school and had the necessities, but they did nothing to prepare me for life outside of the system. I didn't apply to a single college or job and I had no clue as to what to do next. I asked the counselor about a place that took in adults like me and she gave me a list of homeless shelters in the state.

I bounced around to all of the different shelters in hopes to find a more permanent home. Some of them were nice and clean, while the majority of them were dirty and smelled of urine. I assumed the shelters would be like the foster homes, but for adults. It came as a complete surprise when I woke up after the first night at a shelter and was being told that I needed to leave. The shelter was a soup kitchen during the day and I would need to leave. I complied with the order to get out during the day and came back that night. What I was greeted with was yet another surprise. The entrance to the shelter was locked and outside of the door stood a long line full of folks. Some of them I had seen in the shelter last night and others were new. Not thinking anything of it I walked up to the door.

I heard someone yell, "Hey you can't cut the line. You gotta wait just like the rest of us!" I didn't understand what he meant. I wasn't cutting the line, I lived here. I might not be able to be in the shelter in the day, but last night I got a bed here, so I live here.

One of the counselors came to the door to see what the commotion was. I was relieved to see him. He would explain to everyone that I had a bed there; therefore, I lived there and didn't have to wait in a line. My knight in shining armor soon turned into a toad. "I'm sorry ma'am but you are going to need to get to the back of the line." I was shocked. Why did I have to wait in line to get into my new house? He explained to me that no one had a secure spot and they ran the beds on a first come, first serve basis. I had to get in line and wait my turn, hoping that they wouldn't run out of beds before they got to me. I had been waiting for about an hour before I heard, "I'm sorry folks, no more beds for the night, try again tomorrow." My heart sank to my shoes.

Now I had no place to sleep; I was back on the streets. I didn't want to attempt to get a bed in the shelter again so I decided to get a job so I could make enough money to get a place of my own. Following the advice of someone I had met on my journey, I went down to the temporary agency. I was able to get jobs, but they weren't jobs making me enough money to survive, I was going to need to do something else.

My mother's genes must have kicked in because I started stealing. Not credit cards like her, I just stole the necessities. But unlike my mother, I was really bad at it. It wasn't long before I was caught stuffing a pair of jeans into a purse that I stole from the same store a week before and was thrown in jail.

That first night was horrible. I just knew that I was going to wake up to someone attacking me or trying to rape me like I had seen in the movies, but none of that happened. Due to it being my first charge and that it wasn't a violent act, I landed in a minimum-security jail. It was clean and I even had a cellmate that was around my age. She was in for a possession charge. I might have lived on the streets, but I vowed to stay away from the drugs. I knew their power on someone and knew that they turned saints into the devil's minions with ease. I didn't want any parts of that.

The jail was required to serve us three meals a day, something that was never promised to me living on the streets. Even if there would be someone watching my every move, it was a price that I gladly paid. I was safe. And I knew that at the end of the night, I would have a place to lay my head without fear of rats or possums.

My cell was cold and the blankets barely reached my ankles, but they were mine. My cell, my blanket, my space. In my entire life, I had never had anything that was just mine. Even in the foster homes, I still had to share things with the other kids. In a way, I think that the foster home was worse than jail. When I was there I still had hope that someday someone would see me and want to take me home. Every time that it didn't happen, my heart broke. In jail, I knew that no one was coming to get me. Strangely, the lack of hope, made for a happier reality; no expectations meant no pain when they fell through.

I served my time with a smile on my face and after ten months, I was released on good behavior. Then I was right back on the streets. I was back to a place where I didn't know where my next meal would come from or where I was going to sleep. I was back to a place where I had no place to shower or no books to read. I was back to a place that I did not want to be. I knew that I had to get back into jail.

I had too much of a conscience to commit any major crimes, so I stuck with the small stuff. A petty theft charge here and there kept me from living on the streets. After about eight times in the courtroom, the judge told me that if she saw me again, I would serve real time. I couldn't control my excitement; if she gave me real time in jail then I wouldn't have to keep committing crimes to end up there. I was about to tell her that I was 100% fine with that, until she finished what she was saying. "If I see you in here again Miss you will serve real time in a prison, not a jail."

Nash

I had heard the horror stories about prison from people on the streets. They were overpopulated and under staffed. They told me that in prison, there would never be a few days that would go by without someone getting raped. The movies never showed how a woman could rape another woman, but I didn't want to find out. I knew that the judge was serious and I couldn't risk going to prison, but I also couldn't handle life on the streets. I packed up everything that I owned and started walking. I just had to get far enough away that when I got arrested again there would be no way for the judge to act on her threat.

Chapter Nine - Part Three

"Why not just get a job instead of stealing? At least then you could save up to get a shitty place."

"Well Tori I didn't know how to get a job."

"You didn't know how to get a job? Who doesn't know how to get a job?"

"Someone who was never taught. I ended up going to school with the rich kids. They didn't have to worry about getting a job because when they graduated they went to work for the family business or went off to college. I went into the family business too; it just wasn't the same type of business."

"Would your mother really want you to be in and out of jail?"

"She lost the right to tell me what to do when she went to jail."

"What do you mean she lost the right? That is your mother, child! She carried you even after what she went through."

"Yeah and then she went to jail. The stories that she told me are just that, stories. I don't believe that she ever truly loved me and I can't honestly say that I blame her. Every time she looked at me, she probably had flashbacks of being attacked. Who in their right mind would want a constant reminder of their worst nightmare?"

"Have you ever thought about going to see her in jail so she could talk to you and explain that she loves you no matter how she got you?"

"I have actually. There is a big problem with that plan though."

"What's the problem?"

"My mother was released from jail when I was twelve years old. The judge told her where I was and she never came to see me. She was happy that she had me out of her life. Mother or not, some people just don't know how to love. Personally, I never did anything to her and I wanted nothing more than for my mother to love me. I wanted nothing more than for her to tell her friends that she was proud to have me as a daughter and get mad when I didn't talk to her for more than a day or two. First lesson of growing up, you can't always get what you want."

At that very moment I remembered what Lily said to me after my first day here, "the silent treatment? Oh, that is going to be heavenly once they start talking. You still look at them as things in your way to freedom. When those "things" start showing you their humanity, you are going to be in for a rude awakening." She was right yet again. I killed a man and never questioned who was going to miss him, or what caused him to be homeless. To me, he was just trash on the streets that the dumpster man failed to carry away that morning. He was a human and I never lost sleep about taking his life. I never sought forgiveness; I did not even go to his funeral. I was not sure if they even had a funeral for him. Who in the hell was I to play God?

"I would never willingly go to jail."

Tori interrupted my thought process and I was surprised that she held off talking for this long. She was always commenting on the lives and actions of everyone else.

"Look Tori don't start on the judgments."

"I'm just saying, Naomi."

"That's right, you're just saying. You are always just saying things about everyone else's life but yours. What is your story Tori? What are you hiding?"

"Wouldn't you like to know?"

"Yes. That's kind of why I asked the question."

"No one in this room is ready for that answer."

Time had run out for today, but I could not help but wonder the answer myself. Maybe she was a serial killer on the run or a jewel thief. She has a strong personality and broad shoulders; maybe her secret was that she was born a man. What exactly was Tori hiding?

Chapter Ten

I was still running off of the excitement of hearing everyone talk to me today. Sebastian was still acting like a queen so I barely saw him. He would spend his free time either tucked away in his game room or in the home office. He would say that he was working, but I could hear Tony's voice and my imagination would run. Part of me wanted to just bust in on them with a bat, destroy the room and leave, but I could not do that. I had been treating him horribly for quite some time now; I deserved everything that he was doing to me. Plus, where would I go afterwards?

Right now I just wanted to be around noise and people to silence my imagination so I grabbed my things and left. Sadly, at midnight on a Tuesday, there were not very many places to go in my town. I decided on running into the 24-hour grocery store, grabbing a bottle of wine or two, and renting a movie. I could not remember the last time that I drank wine that had a price tag on it or even rented a movie, but I was actually excited about tonight.

As I was leaving the store I heard a familiar voice.

"Hey doc."

I turned around and saw that it was James picking up trash in the parking lot.

"Hello James. What are you doing here?"

"They needed someone to clean up the parking lot tonight and I only have enough meds for the next two weeks so I need the money. What are you doing here?"

I lifted my bag of wine and rentals.

"I was feeling like a night in."

"I would have never pegged you for a store wine and rental type of woman."

"I actually am not one, but I needed a distraction for tonight."

He grabbed my hand and lifted it up.

"Your husband not a big enough distraction?"

"He is probably going to be with his boyfriend tonight."

"Damn. I totally forgot. I'm such a dick."

"It's ok. It has taken me some time to get used to it."

"Well you still shouldn't be out at night by yourself; you could run into a crazy homeless guy like me."

"Very funny. You turned out not to be so bad, so I guess I am willing to take that chance."

"I guess so. Well you be safe out here doc."

"You do the same James."

I turned my back to him and started walking away. I was almost to my car when I realized that the shelter was about a thirty minute drive from here. Who knows where he would be sleeping tonight.

"Hey James!"

"Yeah?"

"I do not know the proper way of asking you this, but I also know that you are not going to walk back to the shelter tonight; I have a few empty rooms if you want to crash tonight."

"You're not afraid that I'm going to attack you in your sleep and rob you?"

"Not anymore."

"Ok. Well I have to finish up here but I would really love that. My favorite alley will probably be all booked up by the time I get off."

"Go ahead and finish up. I'll take these things to my home and come back here in an hour or so."

"Sounds good to me."

I got in my car feeling even better about tonight. Now, not only would I be enjoying some things that I have not had in a very long time, but I would also have someone to enjoy them with. I returned to the house and realized that I had failed to eat the entire day and now it was catching up with me. I wondered if James had eaten today and if he would not mind having dinner with me as well. It had been so long since I cooked for someone other than myself. I felt something light would work best, so I grabbed the shrimp, scallops, Alfredo sauce, pesto sauce, spices, and pasta. It would take about 45 minutes to get everything done and I did not want to look like I bailed on picking James up so I decided that I would just cook and go back to the store. I could shower after we got back.

"Hey, you actually came back."

"I am working on committing to the things that I say."

"I see. Congratulations on that, looks like it's going well for you."

"Thank you. All set?"

"Yes ma'am."

When we got in the car, I started to get a little nervous; this was a guy whose name I just learned today. James, on the other hand, felt completely comfortable. He got in the car and immediately took control of the radio. Apparently, the station that I had on was not good enough.

"Is this what you do whenever you get into someone else's car? Change the station?"

"Well in my Porsche, my driver usually has my favorite station playing. See I like to call them and let them know that I'm tuning in so they play everything that I like."

"Oh, is that right?"

"Yeah totally. I'm kind of a big deal."

"Nice."

It was almost like he did not realize that he was homeless; like he had become so accustomed to the lifestyle that he was not ashamed of it anymore. I could not imagine the stress that I would have if I was in his situation. I would more than likely have gone crazy. Technically he was certified crazy, but even that did not seem to bother him. James just went through life with a smile on his face no matter what. I might have been a tad bit jealous of his ability to do that.

"Ok here we are."

"Hmm. It doesn't look too different from what I imagined it would."

"You imagined what my house looked like?"

"Maybe a time or two. I figured it would resemble the rest of the houses on this side of town; big, brick, warm. Well I assume that it's warm on the inside."

"I guess you will just have to come inside and see for yourself. Are you hungry?"

"I could eat."

"Good. Right this way."

I could tell that James was not used to being in a house like this but he stayed true to his personality and played it cool; joking how my Picasso was clashing with the Feng Shui of the room. I didn't even think to ask if he had any allergies or liked seafood before I cooked. Hopefully he would be ok with dinner.

"Do you like seafood?"

"I'm actually allergic."

"Oh, my gosh I should have asked. I will cook something else. Anything that you want?"

"Doc I'm joking. I love seafood."

"Are you serious at all, about anything?"

"I used to be serious about everything. Then I realized that stressing about everything was killing me quicker than the liquor or the voices so I just stopped. I know that life is clearly not going to be perfect, but that doesn't mean that I have to concern myself with every mistake that I make in life. A turn in the wrong direction just adds to the scenic route to my one day success."

"I guess that makes sense. I wish that I could go a day without stressing. Right about now I would even take an hour of a stress-free mind."

"Well how about this, after dinner I will show you a few of my favorite breathing techniques. They helped me in the beginning."

"Sounds good. Have a seat and I will make you a plate."

"You cooked, bought the wine, and invited me to stay in your home so I would be warm tonight. You have a seat and I will fix the plates. I promise that I won't break anything and if I do, I promise that I will run out of here before you notice."

I imagined him dropping a piece of my crystal and actually running out of here. It made me giggle.

"Ok, deal."

"Thank you."

You would think that he had been in my house before, the way he knew his way around the kitchen. He was able to locate everything with little to no help and carried both of our bowls and glasses of wine to the table with ease.

"You really know your way around the kitchen. Are you sure you have not been here before?" "Please tell me that you are not sleeping with my husband too."

"As flattered as I am that you think your husband would be attracted to me, that isn't my style. I might have lost my mind, but my eyesight is 20/20 and there is nothing I love more than a beautiful woman."

"Ok, ok. I had to ask."

"Most people set up their kitchens the same way, so if you've seen one you've seen them all."

"And here I was thinking that I was original."

"Oh, look who can actually make a joke and I even saw you crack a smile earlier. You should think about doing that more often."

"What? Making jokes?"

"No. Smiling; it looks good on you."

"Thank you."

"No thanks needed. Now dig in. I slaved over a hot stove for this after I got home from a hard day at work."

We laughed and started to eat. When I eat with Sebastian it's usually completely silent, but with James he asked about my day and my past. It was a nice change of pace. After we both had two helpings and finished off the two bottles of wine, he went to the living room to start the movie. About 30 minutes into it I realized that my choice of movies had gotten horrible.

"Am I the only one that thinks this movie sucks?"

"Not at all. I didn't want to say anything because I didn't want to offend your choice in movies, but this is a big bust. I have an idea."

"Anything."

"How about we turn this off and I can show you some of the breathing techniques like I promised."

"Deal."

He put his hands on my chest and my back.

"Is this ok?"

"Yes. it's fine."

It felt nice to be touched by a man, even if it was a homeless one. Strangely enough, I found his cologne intoxicating. It must have been the wine getting to me because what homeless guy maintains his hygiene?

"Deep breaths in, short and quick breaths out. How does that feel?"

"Pretty good. I can feel the tension leaving my back."

"Just like carrying a book bag full of textbooks; the baggage in our lives can be a weight on our backs."

"I did not carry a book bag."

"Then how did you get them to all of your classes?"

"It was mandatory that whoever my boyfriend was at the time, had to carry them."

"Born princess."

"I get it honestly."

"Is that why people like me freak you out so much?"

"I would say that it was part of the reason. Growing up, there were not any homeless people in my neighborhood and the ones on TV did not look very friendly. Sometimes I would run into one when I went to the city, but they just looked dirty and scary. I knew that they were plotting on robbing and killing me, or kidnapping me for the ransom money."

"Boy, do we come from different worlds. In my life, you all are the bad guys. I have been attacked verbally and sometimes physically by the "classy" people driving a foreign car when I was minding my own business. I never understood how the fucked up aspects of my life affected them in such a way that made it ok for them to treat me like trash. You are evidence that people assume that we chose to be homeless, when in reality no one would ever choose to struggle. If battling the weather and other bums wasn't bad enough, most of us have to do it alone. There are very few things in this world that are worse than always feeling alone, no matter how many other bodies surrounded you. I spent my entire life trying to get away from the voices in my head, but it was the real words that people spoke; they broke my spirit in more ways than the voices did."

"Well in the beginning I guess I played right into your expectations."

"Yes, yes you did. Now I see that behind your standoff attitude, was just a scared, miseducated princess. But who am I to judge anyway?."

The idea that I was able to show him that I could be human, really made me excited. Apparently, I was excited enough to drift off into my own little world because James had to wave his hand in front of my face to bring me back to reality.

"Oh, I am sorry, were you saying something?"

"It's cool; I drift off into my own little world too. I was asking if you would mind if I took a shower. I know that you already offered me a room for the night so if I'm pushing my luck, just let me know. I can wait until I go back to the shelter tomorrow to shower."

"No, it is fine. There is a bathroom right down the hall. The towels and washcloths are in the cabinet above the toilet."

"Ok thanks."

"You are welcome."

James had been in the shower for about ten minutes before I realized that he did not have a change of clothes. The whole idea of taking a shower is to get clean so putting on the same dirty clothes once you got out, kind of cancelled out the clean. He was about the same size as Sebastian so I grabbed a grey sweatsuit and a tank top from the dresser. I figured that James would not want to wear another man's underwear so I would just let him wash his so they would be clean.

I knocked on the door to the bathroom, but he did not respond. I could hear the radio playing so he probably would not be able to hear me. I walked in. I would just set the clothes down on the sink and leave. Hopefully he would see them. As I was walking into the bathroom, he was stepping out of the shower. I could tell that he was in good shape, but the oversized t-shirt was hiding an eight pack of abs. I found my eyes staring at his head and making their way down. Thankfully, I was able to snap back to reality before I visually raped him.

"Oh, I am so sorry James, I just wanted to bring you fresh clothes."

I turned my head to face the hallway and held the clothes out with my hand.

"It's cool, no worries. Thank you."

"No problem. I am going to shower now but the washer and dryer are in the room right beside the kitchen. There is detergent in there so you can go ahead and wash your clothes. I could not find any new underwear but I figured that you could wash yours and have them for later."

"Sounds good. Thank you again."

I did not even stay to say you're welcome. The wine was clearly getting to me. I found myself wishing that I had stayed to see him dry off. Come on now Taylor, focus. A nice hot bath would get my mind back on track and off of him. I sat down in the tub and started lathering up my body with the soap. Every time I touched my body I imagined him doing it instead. My hand found its way on the jet again. If I could not get the pictures out of my head, I would just use them for inspiration. I pushed the button but nothing happened. Fuck, my batteries had died. I had been using it a lot these past few days. What was I going to do now? I thought about getting out and looking for more batteries, but the idea seemed like it would ruin the moment. I decided to just finish my bath and get out.

I was walking back downstairs to check on James when I heard the thunder crackle. Now I was completely sure that bringing James home was the right thing to do. He would have had to be outside in the storm. By the look of the sky earlier, I knew that a storm was brewing, but I was hoping that it would hold off. I loved rain storms, but I absolutely hated sleeping alone during them. James must have seen me jump when the thunder cried again.

"Hey are you ok doc?"

“Yes, I am fine. Thunder sometimes scares me and makes it hard for me to sleep alone.”

“Well if you can’t sleep I will stay up with you. I’m sure that there is something to watch on the thousand channels you have on your TV.”

“Thank you, James, I would like that. I am going to fix myself a drink to calm my nerves, would you like one?”

“Who am I to turn down a free drink?”

“I will take that as a yes.”

“It was meant as one.”

To have so many channels, it was pretty hard for us to find a show that we both could agree on to watch. He wanted to watch people blow up and I was more in a love story mood. We finally decided on just watching cartoons. I had forgotten how much I loved cartoons growing up; they were the only things constant in my childhood. The characters wore the same clothes and they came on at the same time every day.

A few hours into our cartoon marathon, I noticed that I could not hear the thunder anymore, and then I noticed the time.

“It is getting pretty late and I think that the storm is over so I am going to head to bed.”

I got up and immediately fell back down. This is why you should not drink sitting down; when you stand up all of the alcohol hits you at once.

“Here let me help you.”

“Thank you.”

"My pleasure."

James helped me up the stairs and into my bed. I stripped down to my t shirt and underwear and he tucked me in. For a moment when our eyes met, I just knew that he was going to try and kiss me, but he just pulled back.

"Good night Dr. Thomas."

"Good night James."

In the middle of the night, I found myself almost jumping out of my skin. The storm had started back up and ruined my sleep. Damn! How am I supposed to sleep like this? With a heart filled with fear and a stomach full of liquid courage, I made my way down the stairs. I knocked on the door to the spare room that James was sleeping in and opened the door.

He was sitting up in the bed; I guess he was not having much luck in the sleep department either.

"Hey I know this is really weird and a bit inappropriate but would you mind if I slept beside you? It is the storm, you know."

"Doc this is your house and technically this is your bed so sleep away."

Thank you.

He lifted the sheets to let me in and moved so that he was sleeping on the top of the sheets. Without them in the way I could see why James was still up. He might have been one strong cough away from his penis ripping a hole into the sweat pants. I turned my back to him so I would not be tempted to stare.

My tossing and turning must have been pretty extreme. I felt James tap my shoulder.

“Hey do you want to do a few more of the breathing techniques; it seems like you are stressing about something.”

Part of me wanted to let him know that it was the image of his dripping body keeping me up, not stress, but I decided against it.

“Yeah. Sure we can.”

He had his hands on my back and chest again. It felt as nice as I remembered. Without thinking, I turned to face him and kissed him. To my surprise, he kissed back.

“No, no we can’t do this doc.”

“Why not? Technically and medically, you are not my patient, so it is ok.”

“It’s not that.”

“What is it then?”

“You are drunk right now and not thinking at the capacity that you normally are. I don’t want you to wake up and regret what we did.”

“I can promise you that I would not regret it.”

“No, you can’t…and I can’t expect you to.”

The rejection had taken away any of the liquid courage that I had left over. I turned my back to him and laid back down to go to sleep.

“Hey, I just said that we shouldn’t have sex. That doesn’t mean that you have to sleep all the way over there.”

“Do you want me to go back to my room?”

"No. I want you closer."

He pulled me up and put me on his chest. Most of the guys I was in bed with, would just have sex with me, and turn over and go to sleep, I am not sure if I had ever cuddled with a man. I could hear his heartbeat; it sounded familiar and I tried to think about what song it matched. He kissed my forehead and said good night. I could not want him more, if I tried.

Chapter Eleven

I woke up to my chin being lifted. I opened my eyes just in time to see our lips meet. He kissed me and the flood gates opened.

“James what are you…”

“Are you completely sober?”

“Yes, I am; why do you ask?”

“Will you remember this in the morning?”

“Yes, I will.”

He kissed me again. I knew that between the liquor from last night, and good ole morning breath, I was not the best candidate for a make out session, but he did not seem to be bothered by it. He kissed me like he was attempting to collect my soul.

“Tell me you want it.”

My heart stopped at the idea. I did not want anything more than to be with him right now. “He moved my hair out of the way and started to kiss my neck.”

“Tell me you want it.”

I could not believe what was happening. Ethics were thrown out of the window the moment I saw him getting out of the shower, so why not get what I want.

“I want it.”

“Louder. Tell me you want it.”

“I want it!”

That must have been the magic volume. James threw the covers off of us and onto the floor.

“What are you doing?”

“We don’t need those. I want to see every part of you.”

He turned me on my back and slid my panties to the side. He licked two of his fingers and gently slid them into my vagina as he kissed my neck.

“Fuck.”

“That’s right doc, let me know that you like it.”

Somehow he knew my body better than I did. His fingers felt so much better than my own. He took them out and put them to my lip.

“Taste them.”

“What?”

“I said taste them.”

He licked his fingers, then put them back on my lip. I licked them like he did, and he kissed me again. This time he did not stop there. He moved his way down to my breasts; first kissing them through my t-shirt, then taking my shirt off. He sucked and nibbled on my breast to the point that I could not hold it in any longer.

“Shit. I’m cuming, I’m cuming.”

I thought that he was done with me, so I lifted up so I could get at a good angle to help him cum, but he had other plans. He pushed me back down onto my back.

"No ma'am. I am not done with you yet. I am starving."

I wondered why he was thinking of food at a time like this, but after the way he made me feel, I did not mind cooking breakfast.

"What do you want to eat?"

He chuckled and started to kiss me again. This time he went from my lips down to my waist. He grabbed my waist with one hand and lifted me up, taking my panties off with the other. Using only his tongue, he traced my vagina slowly, while rubbing on my clitoris with his palm. I could feel another orgasm building and I must have had it written on my face. He took his palm off and lifted up.

"Not yet. I want to taste it."

He took his t- shirt off and dived head first into my vagina.

"Shit. Oh, my fucking…"

The jet had nothing on what James was doing down there now. I could feel his wet rugged tongue going in and out of my vagina.

He moved his hands from my waist to my breast, massaging my nipples. I could feel him nibble a little on my clitoris. At first it was painful, but then I liked it. I knew that I could not hold on much longer.

"James move, I am about to cum."

He grabbed my hands and put them on his head.

"Oh, fucccckkk."

I had never experienced this feeling before. I was in a whole new world until James snapped me out of it.

"Do you have a condom?"

"No. My husband and I have not had sex in quite some time."

"We can stop now then if you want."

James was still wearing the sweatpants. His penis stared at me and I could not help but wonder if he could work it the way he worked his fingers and his tongue. I knew that I should stop, but curiosity was going to win this battle.

"No, it's fine. Just be careful."

"Are you sure?"

"Yes."

"Turn around, get on all fours."

I obliged. As I was turning, he was slipping out of his sweats. I turned my head to be greeted with a beauty. He kept the hair down there tamed and he was circumcised. The overall size was one that could compete with some of my favorite adult stars.

"Turn your head around."

He lifted my hips higher and bit my butt. Then he started with his tongue at the bottom of my vagina, and ended up French kissing my butthole. He was so good with that tongue of his that I almost forgot that he also had a penis attached to him. I was quickly reminded when he began slowly sliding his thick penis, teasing me more and more with every inch.

"Fuck, tell me how that feels. Tell me how that dick feels inside of you."

"It feels good."

He grabbed a handful of my hair and pulled me up by it. He nibbled on my ears and kissed down my neck.

"Tell me how that dick feels."

"It feels so good!"

"That's right. Scream while you cum on this dick."

On a daily basis, James was goofy and a little shy, but sex brought out his inner beast. His beast brought out one in me that I didn't even know I had. I bent back as far as my spine allowed, grabbing and licking on his neck.

"Turn around; I want to watch you take this dick."

I turned onto my back and he bent over to kiss me. He kissed down to my neck, on to my breast, then back to my neck. He made his way to my ear, licking on it and then he whispered,

"Are you done taking this dick or you want more?"

"I want more. I want more!"

"Anything for the good doctor."

He lifted up and began stroking his penis in and out of my vagina. He pulled all the way out, gave my clitoris a lick, and put it back in. The stroking got faster and faster. I lifted up and latched onto his back with my nails. The beast in me wanted to mark her territory on his back.

"Damn you about to make me nut."

"Oh, fuck."

"Nah, not yet."

He pulled all of the way out and laid on his back.

"Come sit on this dick."

I had never tried that position and was nervous about trying it now. I knew that I could not admit that to him, so I just went for it. I held his penis in place with my hands and threw my left leg on his other side. I lifted up above his penis and slowly slid it into my vagina.

"Ahh, ahh!"

"That's right, take all of this dick."

When his penis was fully inside, I started grinding back and forth.

"Oh, shit. Yeah just like that."

I was happy to see that watching porn had come in handy. I wanted to go faster, but I was not sure of how far I could bend on his penis before it became uncomfortable for him.

"Yeah grind on this dick like you love it. You love this dick, don't you?"

"Mmm yes!"

"Yes, what?"

"Yes, I love this dick!"

He lifted me up by my waist and held me in midair while he lifted himself up and down. I looked down at his face and he licked his lips. It was so sexy and I felt another build up.

"Oh, damn I am about to cum again!"

"Nah wait on me doc. Wait on me and we can cum together."

He put me down and flipped me on my back. He lifted my right leg and turned diagonal to my body. That was another position that was new to me. I could not hold it in any longer.

"I'm cuming, I'm cuming! Oh, fuck I'm cuming!"

"Fuck I am too! Tell me where you want it. Tell me where you want to catch this nut."

No man had ever asked me that before so I was not sure of what I should say. Most of the porn I had been watching, he would cum on her face or breasts. On my breasts seemed like a safer choice.

"On my breasts."

"Yes ma'am."

"He pulled out of my vagina. With his hand rubbing up and down his penis he put the top of it in the middle of my breast."

"Fuck yes. You so fucking sexy doc."

He coated my breast with his semen and pulled back. He got off the bed and picked up his towel. It was still damp from his shower earlier and he came back over to me. He wiped up the mess and kissed me. I was expecting him to go take a shower, get dressed, and leave but instead, he climbed back into the bed. He put my head back on his chest and kissed my forehead.

None of the guys I ever had sex with before stayed in bed with me after we were done. It felt nice. I knew that eventually this dream would end and I would have to wake up, but for right now, it felt nice.

Chapter Twelve

It had been over a week since we had our night together, and even though James and I saw each other every day, he never made it awkward. I just knew that he would go back to the shelter and tell everyone what a slut I had been, but he did not. We conversed the same way we did before that night. However, I still feared that someone would figure it out. Someone would notice that my eyes lingered a little too long and then my new secret would be out. I would have to face their judgmental stares for months and months.

“Good afternoon Dr. Thomas.”

“Good afternoon Lily, I mean Dr. Green.”

On my road to being human I had decided that I would treat Lily with the respect that she deserved as well. Who was I to talk down to her? She had the same amount of education as I did, but she obtained it knowing that she wanted to help people. I went to school knowing that I wanted to make my dad happy. A happy dad meant an open wallet.

“Either one works. How are you feeling today?”

“I am feeling fine, why do you ask?”

“No reason. You seem to have this new glow about yourself.”

“Glow? What glow? I do not have a glow.”

"Ok, ok, I'm sorry. You don't have a glow."

"Thank you. Now if you will excuse me, I have a session to get to."

Lily stepped to the side and motioned her arm to the hallway. "By all means. Enjoy your day."

"You do the same."

A new glow? I could not help but wonder if she knew what happened. Why else would she say that I had a new glow? My thoughts were immediately interrupted. I could hear the yelling as I walked down the hallway. It was Tori's voice, but the voice that she was arguing with was not one that I recognized.

"Don't attack me about not letting you guys into my life when you sit there in your chair every day, never saying anything!"

"I might not say anything about myself, but I also have enough respect not to say anything about anyone else's life either."

"So, that makes you better than me?"

"Yes, actually."

No one had ever put Tori in her place so it was nice to see. She was just so strong willed and stubborn that people never wanted to fight with her.

"How about you both calm down?"

"I'm cool, calm and collected doc."

"Ok that is what I want to hear. And you are sir?"

"Name's Garrett."

“Nice to hear your voice Garrett.”

“Thank you. I wasn’t going to participate at all, but I am so tired of hearing Tori talk.”

In my mind, I could not have been more thankful for someone coming along and breaking up the Tori show, but I could not say it out loud.

“Are you fighting with her just to fight, or did you want to share your story?”

“I’ll talk and share whatever you want as long as it means Tori has to give her mouth the day off.”

Tori glared at him and smacked her teeth.

“Go on Garrett, we are listening.”

“Thanks doc.”

GARRETT

I guess I can pinpoint that my story started when my father came back from his first deployment. I had to have been around seven years old and he had been gone for eighteen months. I knew that he was a soldier, a hero, but I also knew that I just wanted him to be my father. At that age, I figured it was ok to be selfish and want him home every night. It was especially hard during father/son games when all of my friends would have a partner and I was alone. My mother said that she would play with me or get my uncle to play with me, but I just wanted my dad.

When he initially sat us down and told us that he would be deployed, the amount of time didn't seem so long. A year and a half, I could handle not seeing my father for that short amount of time. It was not until he left and the time started to pass that I realized how long it actually was and how much things could change.

Physically, things weren't that different. I grew about an inch, my younger sister's hair grew and my mom said that her blood pressure was growing. I wasn't sure what she meant by that at the time. I figured more was always better so it must have been a good thing. I lost a tooth during one of my football games, but for the most part I was the same son that he left behind; we all were the same people that he left behind.

The day came to go pick him up from the airport and we were armed with signs and balloons. I was the first one to spot him, even before he could grab his bags my arms were latched around his waist. Happily, he scooped me up. I lost my hold on the balloons, they flew up and got caught on one of the fans. They popped. Immediately, my father slammed me on the ground and threw his body on top of mine. "Stay down son! They are coming for us! Battles retreat!!"

The entire airport stopped and stared at us while he anxiously surveyed the room as I lay under him crying. Why was he doing this? I couldn't figure out what I had done wrong for him to attack me like this.

My mother ran to us and crouched down to where I could see her face. I could tell that she wanted to cry, but instead she wrapped her arms around my father and whispered in his ear. "It is ok baby. You are safe now, we are safe now. You are home my love…it's ok." I couldn't see my father's reaction, but I could feel the tears drop on my neck. He got up and then picked me up. I turned around to face him and he noticed that my mouth was bleeding. When he slammed me on the ground I bit my tongue. The sight made him cry even harder.

"I am so sorry son. I am so sorry son, please forgive me. I will never hurt you again, I promise son. Please forgive me." He hugged me tighter than he ever had before; I could barely breathe. I told him that I forgave him and could feel the burden as it lifted off his heart. I knew that my father would never hurt me on purpose; he loved me. Being back was just new to him; he would be himself again in no time.

The time passed and things started getting back to normal. My father was steady looking for a job so my mother had to continue working, but it was nice to have him home. I had everything I had been missing since my dad enlisted, the security of knowing that both of my parents would be home every night. It was paradise. That was, until it wasn't anymore.

The longer my father went without a job, the more frustrated he became. He had trouble sleeping when he first came home, but now it was a rarity to see him sleep at all. He began to spend less time with the family and more time alone. He would come home after an interview with a bottle of vodka and head straight to his bedroom, never saying anything to any of us. He was like a zombie version of his former self.

On the scattered occasions that he did come out of the house with us was like walking around with a full S.W.A.T team. He wouldn't let us walk under street lights and would pause if he saw any piece of trash floating in the wind. I had no idea why the trash was suddenly so interesting to him.

None of us could walk behind him and any activity that required prolonged sitting was out of the question. No more family outings to the movies or sports games. I could tell that the person he had become was killing the person he once was. I think that he could feel it happening, but he couldn't help it. If someone fights themselves, there can be no true winner. It pained me to see him in such pain; sometimes I couldn't control the feelings and I would cry. I always tried to make sure that I held my tears in until I was in the privacy of my own room, but one day my father heard me.

He kicked down my door and came storming in. "Son what is wrong?! Is someone here? Are you ok?" I assured him that I was ok; just sad. I saw his face turn from worry to disappointment. "You are crying because your feelings are hurt? I saw men that were like my brothers blown to bits and didn't shed a tear, but you can't control sadness. That's a female emotion anyway so lock that up soldier." Still sniffling I told him that I didn't know if I would be able to. Soon as those words left my mouth I saw his face change again; now he was angry. "What the hell do you mean you don't know if you can control it!? I don't have the patience to wait for you to grow some balls and become a man so I am going to need you to lock it up immediately! What if I were to get hurt in the war? How could I possibly leave the family in the hands of a pussy?" It was then I realized without a shadow of doubt that the father that left for the military was not the father that came back.

My mother apparently noticed it as well. She started to come home later and later to avoid being in the same room with my father for extended periods of time. It wasn't soon before my father realized what she was doing as well. My life changed drastically the night he confronted her about it.

I was in my room, but I could hear my father yelling at my mom. "Why are you coming home so late? Where have you been?" My mother brushed him off and went into the kitchen. "Did you hear me woman!?" His voice was growing louder and she was still ignoring him. I heard a crash, then my father yelling again, and then nothing at all. I sat frozen on my bed; something wasn't right. Against my better judgment I walked out into the living room. The room was still.

I knew that I was walking towards the kitchen, but I couldn't actually feel my feet moving. My heartbeat grew faster and faster while the rest of the world seemed to freeze. My stride was interrupted by something on the floor, I looked down. My mother lay on the ground by my feet, her once brown and joy filled eyes, were now cold and filled with anguish. I looked around to see if anyone else noticed my mother's condition, but the house was empty. My father had taken my baby sister and fled the scene.

I called the police and reported that my mother had been murdered and that the only suspect was long gone. The fact that he had taken my sister along made it a hostage situation and they had to act accordingly. An Amber alert was sent out and the calls started to flood in. Most of the calls weren't useful, but the station did receive a call that explained everything.

Apparently, someone that my father fought beside called with monumental concern. He told the officers that my father had talked about going to a lake house once they returned home. In addition, he told them that he was surprised that my father was able to come home untreated in his condition.

My family and I had assumed that my father came back home because his deployment was over but in actuality, he was kicked out. During a routine psych evaluation, the doctors diagnosed my father with severe PTSD and he was medically discharged. No one thought that it would be a good idea to tell us of his condition; they just signed his papers and released him into an unsuspecting world. The signs were there; we all knew that he wasn't the same man as before, but no one knew exactly what was wrong. If we had known, we could have gotten him help. If we had gotten him help, I could have still had my family alive and well.

One positive thing that I could say about the military after all of this, they trained my father well. The local and federal police searched for months and didn't get one solid lead. As the months turned into years everyone turned to different cases and my mother's case went cold. They had given up and I began to move on.

My uncle took me in and I adjusted to my new life. My uncle made sure that I went to school every day and kept my grades up. A month before my graduation my uncle sat me down at the kitchen table and placed two sets of papers in front of me. One set was college applications and the other was enlistment papers. "Pick one nephew." I told myself that after I witnessed what the military turned my father into that I would steer clear, but there was nothing about college that interested me. Reluctantly, I chose the enlistment papers.

The ink was dry and I had been sworn in; there was no turning back now. Boot camp turned out to be a breeze for me. My father raised me to be strong and determined, so anything that I put my mind to and my heart into, I accomplished. Although I could handle it, my first time home after boot camp came as a true relief and a welcoming break from my new life. It was good to see everyone that I loved all in one place again. Since my father took my sister, I had a new outlook on family and a strengthened protection for the ones I love.

After my quick stay was over it was back to my military lifestyle. My assignment was to be stationed in Tennessee for a couple of years as I continued my training. Everything was going fine until my name was called one day during a meeting. They told me that I had been chosen for deployment… my heart sank into my shoes. I was not 100% sure of how my deployment would go, but I knew that when my father went he never came back.

I knew that I didn't have a choice so I just started to get ready the best way I knew how. I prayed and I worked out more than ever. The idea was that if I kept my body strong it would keep my mind strong too. I refused to let this deployment turn me into my father. I simply refused.

A year after being deployed I was given the option to continue in the military or hang it all up. When I chose to enlist instead of going off to college, I made a commitment to myself to stay active for at least fifteen years. I wanted the experience and I wanted to stay in longer than my father. After I came back from deployment, my plan changed…I was done. I saw things that no one should ever see. I saw civilians caught in the crossfire and blown to bits on the streets. It finally made sense why my father would stop for random pieces of trash flowing in the wind. A simple piece of road side trash proved to be an IED, or homemade bomb. I saw one blow up on a group of children playing tag. They could not have been any older than nine or ten years old; they didn't even know that it was a war going on. That day their young lives were ended far too soon and it took my passion for this lifestyle with it. My heart couldn't take this happening again, so when the decision came, I retired. Once I was done with the military portion of my life, I turned to college. I might not be a fan of classes and due dates, but at least I knew that I wouldn't have to witness a soul leaving another body. Not again.

College went by smoothly; I even found a girl and we fell in love. She was the first woman that I had been able to love since losing my mother. I vowed that I would never hurt her the way that my father hurt my mother. I may look like him and I may have been in the military like him, but I am not my father. My girlfriend would ask about my family, but I always dodged the question. If I told her the truth about my family she would look at me and see my father. She would see a man that was able to kill a woman he vowed to cherish.

The time flew by and our love grew. I didn't think that I could be any happier until she told me that we would be having a baby. It was finally my chance to show everyone that I was better than my father in every way. I knew that I wanted to bring my baby into a loving family; I asked her to marry me. She said yes. A few months later, she gave birth to my beautiful baby girl and about a year after, we were married.

I started to see my sister in my daughter and it would automatically take me to a place I didn't want to be. Why couldn't I have saved my sister? I was some big strong soldier now able to fight for my country, but I couldn't even protect my sister. Every time that my daughter cried my heart would break and I would run to her, apologizing for not protecting her and reassuring her that I would let anyone hurt her again.

The more protective I tried to be, the more paranoid I got. The more paranoid I got, the more I felt like my father…I guess the apple didn't fall too far from the tree. When my wife would do something to upset my daughter, I would picture hurting her. The pictures became more and more vivid until one night I packed up a bag and walked out of the house. I knew that if the visions were there the actions would follow. I loved my family far too much to hurt them, but I couldn't control myself for much longer. I removed myself from the equation and even if they did not understand why I left, they would be alive to not understand it. Walking away before it turned ugly made me a better man than my father.

Chapter Twelve - Part Two

My initial reaction was shock. For a man who spent most of his time just listening, he had quite a story to tell.

"That doesn't explain how you ended up on the streets."

"Well, Dr. Thomas once I lost my family, I lost my everything. I didn't want to do anything or go anywhere, so life on the streets just seemed like the easiest solution."

"So, you are basically a homeless vet because you wanted to prove your father wrong?" "Yeah, way to go there Garrett."

"Look Tori can you just hush? Is it physically possible for you to engage in listening to someone's life and not give them your two cents? I am not a homeless vet because I wanted to prove my father wrong, I am a homeless vet because I wanted to prove myself wrong. I would have nightmares about transforming into him and when I looked into my daughter's eyes, I could not bear to hurt her. My wife looked at me full of admiration and pride of the man I was, I couldn't take that image from her."

I cannot think of a time that I loved someone strongly enough to give up my dreams for them and here was a man that gave up his entire life for his family. I cannot even begin to imagine what it mentally took for him to walk away from the two women he loved.

"What about your father and your sister?"

"I gave up looking for them years ago Lauren."

"But why? If you really loved them and wanted to see them again you would have never given up."

"Look Lauren. you're still a baby, I don't expect you to understand. Sometimes you run out of options and the only decision left is to quit."

"Look Garrettt, I might be young, but I do understand. I understand that if I lost someone that I loved and I knew they loved me, I would never stop looking for them. Even when you run out of options, you should never run out of hope. New trails present themselves everyday but if you already have that door closed, you'll never see them."

I was surprised to hear such passion and wisdom coming from a teenager. She was a lot quieter than the rest of them but I could tell that she was hiding something. She was hiding something big and it was my duty as the therapist to find out what it was.

Chapter Thirteen

It felt as though Sebastian and I had not spoken in years. My home had transformed into a haunted house. The frigidness of the air pierced through my skin and sliced out any feelings of love that I once had for him. I always knew that my relationship was a business arrangement but seeing Sebastian with Tony made it all far too real. The conversation preceding it did not help at all either. I told myself that Sebastian had to have some type of love for me to marry me but that assumption was smashed by the harsh reality check of our relationship. He did not love me; he probably did not even like me. I was just the prettiest girl in his contact list and maybe that was not even true. Maybe I was just the prettiest girl that was willing to commit her life to being a prop. All that I was to him was a prop, something to show off at company parties so his colleagues would look and comment on how he was a lucky a man.

I was reflecting on life in the kitchen when I heard the front door open.

"Tay, you home?"

I had almost forgotten what his voice sounded like. Was he really looking for me?

"Yes, I am here. I am in the kitchen."I could hear his footsteps growing closer and my throat becoming drier and drier with his every step. Why was he looking for me? What could he possibly want to say to me?

“There you are. Hi Tay, how are you?”

“Umm I am fine. How are you Sebastian?”

“I’m great, magnificent even.”

“Good to hear. You seem to be in a chipper mood today.”

“Oh, I am, I am. Tony and I have decided to rent a lake house together.”

“Oh. Well are you asking me for a divorce?”

“Of course not. You are stuck with me until I am done with you. At least now you won’t have to worry about seeing anything though. Everyone wins!”

He smacked my butt and walked away with that huge grin still on his face. He knew that he had me right where he wanted me. If I were to divorce him, it would be a breach of our contract and I would get nothing. I needed money to maintain my lifestyle so I needed him. I could not get to the shelter fast enough, at least they wanted me around more than my husband did. Who could have guessed that what once was a hell hole for me, was now my safe haven?

Chapter Fourteen

Going to the shelter had converted from a court ordered punishment to a refreshing day to day activity. Everything was just easier there…well almost everything. I could not stop thinking about James and the night we had. I would look at him and immediately flash back to the passion we shared. I wondered if he had told anyone about what happened. I mean he is not really my patient, so no laws were broken but it still would be frowned upon. A rich married psychologist having an affair with a homeless, former mental patient because her secretly gay husband could not bear to touch her again. My world had become a bad script for a TV movie.

"Good afternoon Dr. Thomas."

"Good afternoon Lily."

"How is everything going?"

"Everything is the same."

"Hmm I guess I'll leave it alone."

"Good idea. I am going to my session now. You have a great day."

"You do the same Dr. Thomas."

The building read like a classic novel to me now. The pictures on the wall no longer came as a surprise and the once foul odor was replaced with a comforting scent.

"Hello everyone."

"Hi doc."

"Hello James."

He licked his lips when he said hi and my panties instantly became wet. I could not believe the effect that such a simple gesture had on me. Could they tell where my mind was? I was sure that it was written all over my face.

"You guys, I left some paperwork in my car, so I am just going to go back and grab them."

The reality of the situation was that my lust for James at the moment was overflowing. There was no way that I would be able to continue this session without relieving myself. The bathroom was too open but my car was parked in the back where the lights were low and I could get some privacy.

I quickly made my way to my car and got into the backseat. I had never done this in my car before but I was out of options. I nervously pulled off my panties, placed them on the floor and put one of my legs on the back of the driver's seat and the other on the passenger seat; carefully watching that no one came outside. I felt as though this was the safest it was going to get so I started to rub my breasts. My nipples were tender and sensitive; I almost had an orgasm just by licking my fingers and touching them. I was making my way to my vagina when I heard a knock on my front window. I froze. Who was at my car? What all had they seen?

I got up and pulled my dress down before rolling down my window just far enough to see who it was. It was James. What did he want? I rolled down the window a little further so that I could ask him.

"Hi, umm hi James. How can I help you?"

"Hey doc. I'm not out here to ask for your help. I saw the look on your face in the room before you left. I know that look…I created that look. I came out here to help you."

Before I could respond he had opened the driver's door and climbed into my car.

"What, what are you doing?"

"Put your legs back up like you had them."

"You saw that?"

"Put your legs back up like you had them."

I complied. It was something about James that was so intoxicating that I would do just about anything he asked. I lifted my legs back up and he took his shirt off. He leaned into the backseat and kissed me. I was not sure if it was his chest pressing against mine or the pure stare of lust in his eyes when he kissed me, but I melted from the inside and it leaked onto my seats. He must have felt it happen because he looked down and chuckled.

"Doc I haven't even done anything yet."

He leaned forward on my chest and whispered in my ear.

"You must have missed me."

There was no hiding the fact that I did in fact miss him. Beyond the amazing sex, I missed the gratification that just having him in my presence provided me. The feel of his tongue inside of me snapped me back to reality.

“Oh, m   y.”

He lifted his head up showing with a face of arrogance. A cocky attitude would usually turn me completely off but everything looked better on James.

“Yeah you missed me. You missed me and I’m going to make you show me just how much.”

He slowly put two fingers in my vagina and started to massage my walls. I bit on my bottom lip in attempts to smother my moans.

“Oh, no ma’am. I wanna hear you.”

James french kissed my clitoris and I could not help but let out my moan.

“There you go doc. You know how I like it.”

I could not believe that I was doing this again and in the parking lot of a homeless shelter! What in the world is wrong with me? It felt so good to have a man that wanted me and everything that included. I think that I had fallen in lo…

“Oh, my goodness!”

While I was trying to figure out what was wrong with me, James was continuing to prove what was right with him. I opened my eyes to find him on top of me. He had pulled his pants down and pushed his penis through his boxers. I latched my nails into his back as he dug deeper into me, the deeper I dug into him.

“You’re going to mark me up.”

"Oh my word! I'm sorry, I will stop."

"No. Don't stop!"

The moans from our mutual orgasms filled my car and fogged my windows. I would have loved to stay and soak up each other's juices, but I had already been out of the session too long. I had to think about how I would explain what took me so long.

"You go in first and I will be back in later."

"You got it doc."

He kissed me one last time and disappeared back into the shelter. I surveyed my car for papers that could pass as being important but it was a bust. I decided that I would take a quick trip to the copy store and make up something that looked good.

With a few sprays of perfume and newly copied papers in hand I went back into the building. I did not want to take a chance at Lily seeing my face and mentioning a glow again so I just kept my head down and headed back to the session.

"Damn doc did you have to cut down the tree and make the paper yourself?"

"No Tori, I did not. I left the papers in my home office and had to drive back to get them."

"Home office? Of course, you have a home office. How could you not have a home office?"

"This is not about me Tori. If you want to talk about anything, how about you talk about yourself?"

"Hmmm, yeah no."

“Of course, you do not want to share. Well, does anyone else want to share their story? Wait, I think we may have heard from everyone except for Tori.”

“I haven’t shared.”

“I looked around the room to see who said that.”

“Down here.”

I had forgotten about Lauren. The only time that I had heard her talk was when she was confused about James being jealous of people in wheelchairs. She looked so young. It saddened me to think that she lost the ability to walk before she got the chance to really start her life. If being homeless at a young age was not bad enough, she was bound to a chair as well. I was curious about how she ended up here.

“Hi. Lauren, right?”

“Yes, that’s right.”

“Well, Lauren go right ahead. You have the floor; what’s your story?”

LAUREN

Dance, sing, act, sports, etc; when I was younger, I did it all. I just loved competition and being on stage while everyone gawked at me. I would have liked to say that I didn't let the attention go to my head, but it would be a humongous lie. I knew that I was one of the best and I had no problem telling the world that.

My cockiness was fine when I was five and six but the older I got the more annoying my cocky attitude became. I could feel people grow uninterested as I would gloat but I couldn't stop it. Everyone had to know that I was the best. I mean, what was the point of winning if no one knew? Anytime there was a group of people around me, there was an audience and every audience needs a star. I was that star.

On my thirteenth birthday, my mom sat me down and explained to me that I had to discover humility because the older I got the more trouble my mouth would get me into. I couldn't understand her reasoning behind telling me to hide who I was, when she had always encouraged it growing up. "If you aren't the best you aren't relevant." "Only the winners are remembered." "Only the effort of number one matters; everyone else just wasted their time." My mom said at least one of these quotes to me before every competition. She created the egotistical monster and now she wanted me to change. I couldn't. I wouldn't.

My family ended up moving to a different state prior to me starting high school. In high school, the competition level skyrocketed. I was used to competing with girls my age, but now

I would have to go up against seventeen and eighteen year olds, who had been perfecting their craft since they were babies. Needless to say, I was a bit intimidated. I knew that I couldn't let that affect me. Every time I stepped on any stage my goal was to win, they would have to pry the title from my cold hands, regardless of their age.

One day I saw the flyers advertising the fall talent show in the hall. No one there had ever seen me perform, so this was my chance. I skipped lunch and made my way to the office to get more information about it. There was a group of older girls waiting in the office and they saw me sign up. One of them said, "You're wasting your time fresh meat. Krystal always wins." I didn't know, nor did I care, who Krystal was. I replied that if she always wins, then maybe it was time for a change. They giggled and gave the most sarcastic good luck I had ever heard. I didn't need their faith in me, I had faith in me.

The night of the talent show came and I was ready. I peeked out from behind the curtains and saw that it was a full house. I always performed better in front of a lot of people. Being able to feed off the energy of the crowd was my favorite part of being on stage.

We pulled numbers to choose the order, I chose the biggest number so I was last. I just sat backstage and watched everyone else. Most of the acts were pretty mediocre, a spoken word piece here, and a song there. Nothing that I had seen could hold a flame to what I had planned for the night, and then the host called Krystal's name.

She walked onto the stage and a group of six boys and girls followed her. They got in their places behind her and she took place center stage. The spotlight was on her and she took full advantage of it. By the end of her performance, it was obvious why she won every year. She sang and danced like she was getting paid as a professional artist. It was easy to see that she was born to be on stage. I admit that it made me nervous but more importantly, it made me determined. Krystal believed that the stage was hers and I was going to show her that there was a new sheriff in town.

When it was finally my turn, I confidently walked on stage. I knew that I could sing and dance, but now I had to do something amazing to woo the judges in my favor. The music started and the idea hit me like a ton of bricks. Anyone could hide behind a track, or distract the audience with fancy dance moves, but only a true artist could take all of that away and still win. I motioned to the deejay to turn the music off and grabbed a stool from backstage. If I was going to do this I was going to win, I had to win.

I sat on the stool half way and gently held the mic in my hand. This was my moment. All eyes were on me and they wanted to know what an unknown freshman was going to do. In their minds, Krystal had already won and I was just a buffer between her performance and the results. They put the spotlight on me and I could see people beginning to get up and walk out. No one walks out while I am on stage. I opened my mouth and as soon as I released the first note, everyone stopped in their tracks. There that's better, all eyes on me. By the end of my song, people either had their mouths on the floor or their eyes swollen due to them crying; such a beautiful sight. I walked off stage with my head held high, and waited for the judges to calculate their scores. The longest five minutes of my life passed by before they announced that they were ready.

The host called us all back onto the stage. He started to announce the runner ups, but I blocked their names out. I was not here to be a runner up, so those results had nothing to do with me. "And the winner is…after a tight race. The winner is… Lauren!!!" The news brought the audience to their feet and Krystal to her knees. It felt good to know that, not only had I won, but by doing so I knocked the queen clean, smooth off her throne. I may have been fresh meat, but from this moment on, that stage belonged to me.

My win jump started my popularity at school. Everyone wanted to know about the freshman that beat Krystal at her own game. I loved every moment of my new-found attention. It was like being in the spotlight every day. While I was soaking it all up, Krystal was sulking in her loss. I wanted to tell her how much I had enjoyed her performance, but no one had seen her since the show. I would have just said something after the show, but once the results were read she ran off stage. I saw her talking to her mother as I was leaving the theater. I was going to speak, but their conversation looked a bit heated, so I decided against it.

After another successful day at school, I started to make my way home. The fact that I lived so close to the school made it easier to convince my parents to let me walk to and from school every day. Being able to walk alone made me feel like a real adult. They trusted me to get to school on time and get home at a decent time. This particular day, they were doing maintenance on the main road, so I had to make a detour into the woods. I was just at a bonfire in the area so I knew it pretty well. I was upset because I was going to get my shoes dirty so I put my headphones on to make the walk more bearable.

I was about halfway through the trees when an uncomfortable feeling overtook my body. I took my headphones off and called out to see if anyone was there. No answer. I concluded that I was just being paranoid and kept walking.

I still couldn't shake the feeling of being watched, so I began to speed walk and then run through the trees. I took a quick look back behind me to see if anyone was following me and completely failed to notice the huge rock in my pathway. I tripped and my phone smashed between my body and the rock. I picked it up in an attempt to fix it, but it was destroyed. I bent down to grab my headphones and when I stood up something hit me in my head. I passed out.

When I finally came to, I was greeted with darkness. I tried to get up, but my arms were bound behind me. I am claustrophobic, so the tight space made me start to hyperventilate and panic. I heard someone cry "Shut up back there and stop moving! We are almost there and then the real fun will start." That was the moment that I knew I would not make it home and I cried out at the thought.

I could feel the car start to slow down and I braced myself for the monster that was going to open the trunk. I painted the picture of an older man, tall with a stocky build. He would be wearing a black sweat suit and latex gloves. I was a virgin, but if he had kidnapped me he was probably going to rape me too. The life I had planned for myself ended as soon as he hit me in the head. We parked and I heard the engine turn off. This was it. He got out of the car and slammed the door. I counted down the footsteps he had left until he reached the trunk. 3…2…1.

I heard the key turn and the trunk pop open. I closed my eyes tight, expecting to be struck again but I wasn't. "Wakey, wakey sleeping beauty." Just by the voice I could tell that the kidnapper I pictured was not the one that had taken me. I opened my eyes and my chest tightened. It wasn't some crazy old man at all. It was Krystal.

She must have read the confusion on my face. "Aww what's wrong sweetheart? You didn't expect to see such a beautiful angel when you opened your eyes?" I started to open my mouth to ask her why, but she interrupted me. "No, no, no. You have said and done quite enough. Now it's my turn." She helped me out of the trunk and led me to the house. I surveyed the area hoping that something would look familiar, but nothing did.

We made it into the house and she laid me on the kitchen table. I wasn't 100% sure of what she was going to do, but I knew that it would not be pretty. She cut the rope off of my arms and tied them to the table instead. She did the same thing to my legs. Oddly enough, the scariest part during all of it was her face. Here was a high school girl tying me to a table for a reason unknown to me, and she did so with a huge smile on her face.

My mouth was dry but somehow I formed the words to ask her why she was doing this to me. "Why? You want to know why? Well I will tell you. I was a winner! I was a winner and you stole that from me!" This was about the talent show. Everything that my mother said about my cocky attitude getting me in trouble replayed in my head. "Oh nothing to say now, huh?! I get it, you're a winner, why would you talk to a loser?! Why would you waste your breath?" I could hear her pacing back and forth, so I lifted my head to see what she was doing. She had a gun in her hand.

I pleaded to her that this wasn't necessary; even told her that I would give her the trophy. "No! I don't want your stinking trophy! I want to be the best and the only thing standing in my way, is you."

I couldn't control the tears any longer and I let out a high-pitched wail.

"Shut up! Just shut the hell up Lauren!"

I sniffled in attempt to get my thoughts together. I asked her if she was going to kill me. "Kill you, what kind of monster do you think I am? I'm not a murderer; I'm just a winner. After I am done, everyone will forget about you and I will graciously return to my throne."

With that said, she turned to point the gun on my legs.

POW! POW! POW! POW! She put two shots in my left leg and two more in my right. "There, that solves you dancing…now for your singing." She grabbed a scalpel from the counter and put it to my throat. My body quivered but she grabbed my neck and cut me. "There, all done. Not enough to kill you, but just enough to kill your career. Well I'm all done here." She wiped down everything that she touched; I could smell the bleach in the air. "Goodbye Lauren, congrats again on your win."

Just like that, she disappeared outside. I could feel the blood seeping through every injury she made, and I could feel myself slipping away. I knew that I wouldn't make it out alive.

In a freak turn of events, I survived. I woke up to needles in my arm and tubes in my nose. My head was killing me but I could tell that I was in a hospital. The nurse noticed that I had awakened and she went to get the doctor. He came in to check my vitals and asked me a bunch of questions about who I was and how I ended up in the house. I answered them the best way that I could.

"You have been in a coma for five days. You don't have a record and you didn't have any ID on you, so we didn't know your name. Without a name, we couldn't find someone to come get you. Is there someone you would like us to call?"

The first person to cross my mind was my mom. If he called my mom, she would come pick me up and I would be safe. I gave him the number and about an hour later my mom showed up and the doctor came back into the room.

"Her vitals are all good now, you can take her home today." He was talking, but I saw that my mom's focus was on my legs and not on his words. The doctor noticed her as well. "Yes, well, when it comes to her legs, the news is not as good. The bullets paralyzed her in both legs; odds are that she will never walk again." I knew that was coming, but it shocked my mom. As they brought in the wheelchair and the paperwork to sign so I could leave, the shock never left her face. The entire trip was silent.

We turned into a gas station and my mom helped me into my chair so I could go use the restroom. "Go in and get the key; I'm going to put some gas in the car." I rolled my way into the store and got the key. I was already winning at the wheelchair life. When I went back outside, I noticed that the car was gone. Frantically, I rolled to the pump where the car was and found a note. It was from my mother; she wrote, “I can’t take care of you so you must take care of yourself. Good luck.”

Chapter Fourteen - Part Two

I knew that she was hiding something, but I did not think anyone guessed this was the story they would hear from her. My heart ached for her even more now. Was this what it felt like to be human? To have emotions? I can see why I chose a different route for so long. The ability to feel and care about someone other than yourself, just left you open to pain.

"I thought my relationship with my mother was shitty, but what type of mother would leave her child stranded after she almost died?"

"What was your relationship like with your mother Tori?"

"Good try doc, but we are talking about Lauren right now."

Simply mentioning her mother was the first-time Tori even attempted to share something about herself besides her overbearing opinions. I had to try and get more information out from her, but she was right. We were discussing Lauren's story, so Tori's mystery would have to wait.

"I'm sorry I misjudged you."

"It's cool Garrett. Sometimes the story of how we got such a nifty accessory is an accident, other times it's a tragedy. The important thing is that a situation that could have ended my life, merely changed my life. There are still days where I forget that I am even handicapped and try to throw my legs over the bed in the morning and walk to the bathroom. It's not being in the wheelchair that's the hard part; the most heart wrenching pain comes from remembering that I wasn't always like this."

"That might be the most insightful thing I have heard in the sessions."

"Oh, so what the rest of us have been saying is basically going in one ear and out the other?"

"Tori that is not what I said."

"You didn't have to say it directly. I could tell what you were hinting at."

"Tori why do you do this?"

"Do what?"

"You turn everything into a negative and debate that everyone is against you. No one is against you!"

"Yes, yes you are. You are against me and you don't even know it. Hell, you don't even know me."

"And who is to fault for that?"

"Now you are going to blame me because you aren't pushing to hear my story like you did for everyone else?"

"I did not push for any one story more than another. You choose to be closed off. You choose to be judgmental towards everyone. You choose to hide behind your sarcasm, but you know what?...I see you."

Tori let out a hardy laugh that seemed to have formed in the very pit of her soul.

"Oh, you see me now? Well then tell me doc, what do you see?"

"You are a coward. You are so afraid to let people in, that you put up walls every chance you get."

"Afraid to let people in, that's your big diagnosis? You really know nothing about me."

"Well how about you tell me then Tori?"

"Tell you what? My life reeks of desperation…something that you could not relate to."

"I have been desperate before Tori."

"No. Doc you may have been uncomfortable before but you have never been desperate. You don't know what it feels like to be TRULY desperate…to go from wanting to be Mother Theresa to being a prostitute; from being a martyr, to becoming Hitler. You have no idea what it's like to be FORCED to survive. To reconsider every moral you've ever had because they are getting in the way of your survival. There is no stooping too low when the goal is staying alive."

TORI

I am a natural born addict. The obligation for a fix is embedded in me like my eye color or the shape of my ears. My mother was an addict and a prostitute and she passed those traits right on to me. She didn't protect herself when she was "working" and unfortunately, she contracted HIV because of it. She did not take the necessary steps when she found out that she was pregnant, so she gave that to me as well to complete the trifecta of my existence. She didn't give a damn about anyone or anything that wasn't helping her to get her next fix. My mother was a selfish, vindictive woman most of the time. During the rare time that she remembered that humans had feelings, she would share moments when she would smile and lighten the entire room, or speak and it sounded like a songbird. In those moments…she was beautiful.

I never met my father; well then again maybe I did. My mother had no idea who he was and she was angry with him. She wasn't angry because he wasn't there, she was angry because he got her pregnant, and even more angry at me for making her miss out on months of work. For years, I would picture who he was. Would he have hazel eyes like me or did they skip a generation and I got them from his parents? Was he left-handed? I am left-handed, but my mother wasn't. The only joy that came from not knowing who he was, was that I could believe that he was a good man. I could think, that if he knew about me, he would be there; that if he knew about me, he would love me.

I eventually replaced my desire for a father with a desire for a man. There had to be some man out there that loved me, even if my father didn't. Hell, there had to be someone out there that loved me, even if neither of my parents did. As I grew, so did my physique. With booming hips and breasts, I got all the love that I needed.

I was about sixteen the first time I had sex. I had sex with a boy from school. It was painful and I couldn't understand why people made such a big deal out of it. I was ready to make him get up until I looked up into his eyes. The amount of pleasure and concentration on his face screamed love to me. When we were getting dressed, he asked me if I wanted anything before he took me home and it caught me by surprise. No one had ever asked me if I needed anything. No one had ever cared enough to make sure I had completed my homework, or even eaten. But he did. I told him that I was fine, but just the gesture reiterated the idea that he loved me. I finally had someone that loved me.

The next day when I saw him at school, I ran up to him and gave him a hug. I literally felt the temperature drop around me as he slid me off his arms and shoved me away. The look of utter confusion must have been plastered on my face. He looked me straight in my eyes and said, "Thanks for last night, I was wondering how it would be with a virgin." I was just barely able to mutter out a thank you. It was when he turned his back to me and walked away that my entire body became numb. It didn't feel like love anymore and that was the final crack needed to break my heart. If no one wanted to stay in my life, then I would just get what I needed and leave them before they left me. I promised myself that I would never feel broken again. I realized that life was all about playing the game and the game was always take care of yourself first and let the cards fall as they do. My father played the game, my mother played the game, hell, even the dumb ass I let take my virginity played the game, and now I was going to play too.

Boyfriends, girlfriends, younger, older; I was an opportunist. Life was just…well, life for me. I had finally found my escape and I saw why my mother had chosen to make a career out of it; sex solved every problem I had. If I was sad, I would have sex and be happy. If I was low on money, I would have sex and make some. I stayed on top of my meds to maintain my HIV the best I could, and always used protection. I didn't want to curse anyone else the way my mother had cursed me. She lived her life like it had no effect on anyone else. I was born prematurely with a heroin addiction and HIV positive, but she didn't care. My mother was the master at playing the game, I watched her closely because I wanted to be a master too. I wanted to not feel or care about the well-being of anyone other than myself. The sex helped for a while, but when it stopped, I turned to another thing I was born to do. Heroin.

I knew that my mother would be shooting up soon; it was too late in the day for her not to be. Thankfully, I had caught my mother on one of her good days; one of her days when her smile lit up the room. On that day, if you were in her presence, every bad thing seemed to disappear; you just knew that no matter what, things would be ok. She was just tying the rubber around her arm when I walked in. I told her that I wanted to try it. At first, she looked at me and I swear I almost saw an ounce of sorrow, but then, she just shook her head and said, "Oh so you're a big girl now? Selling your young loins for lunch money not getting you your fix anymore, and now you want to try something new?" I stood frozen.

My mother and I didn't talk very much and I felt like any answer that I gave her would be wrong. She would yell at me to get out of her face, or call me everything, but a child of God…but none of that happened. Instead she took the rope off of her arm and motioned for me to sit beside her. She handed me the rope, "you know how to work this thing?" Still afraid that she would lash out at me, I just shook my head no. She chuckled as she rolled up my sleeve and tied the rope on my arm. "Take two fingers and pat your arm until you find a good vein; you're my girl and good veins run in our family so it won't take long."

I did what she said and found a vein in no time. I watched as she lit the bottom of the spoon with the mixture she had made originally for herself, and then sucked it all up into a syringe. She handed me the syringe, "See that vein; that perfect vein you got poking out there? You're going to take this and dive right into that vein with it." My hands were shaking uncontrollably. I tried a few times but couldn't get it to go in. "It's ok baby, mama's got you." She took the syringe back from me and held my arm steady, "see just like this." I watched the heroin disappear into my arm and felt every ounce of worry I had fade away. I turned to look at my mother face to face and whispered, thank you. She had just shot me up with my first taste of voluntary heroin and…I thanked her.

The more heroin I fed into my body, the less I cared about anything else. If it wasn't concerning my next fix, then I just simply did not have time for it. I was still prostituting for money, but instead of fancy clothes and trips, it was going right into my arm. I stopped taking my meds for my HIV because I had a new drug; a better drug. It wasn't about reality anymore. No, it was about making it through the day without having to realize what a complete fuck up I had become. Things that used to be so important to me, just fell flat in comparison to my addiction.

Before, I made sure that every time I "worked," I protected my customer by using a condom. Some would ask to do it without and offer more money, but I knew that I had HIV, even if they didn't. It was my moral obligation. Time passed and I had shot all of my morals away. I started having unprotected sex sometimes with multiple men in one night, sometimes with multiple men at one time. They didn't ask me if I was clean, and I didn't offer up my medical history. I figured that I couldn't get cursed twice and if they really cared about their own lives, they wouldn't put themselves at risk. It wasn't in my job description to be their parent. I just started to move around to different locations so if, and when, they did trace it back to me I would have been long gone.

One day as I was just walking into a hotel room to meet a new client, I felt dizzy. I hadn't shot up for a few hours, so I just figured it was a symptom of withdrawals and I shook it off. In about thirty minutes, I would have the money I needed for a hit, and the dizziness would disappear. I smiled at him as I unzipped his pants, then moved down to do my work as usual, but he stopped me. He grabbed me by my neck and yanked me up so that I was face to face with him. "I'm not paying for you to like this bitch!" I had guys that asked for role playing before so I just shook it off and explained to him the extra price for what he wanted. "This isn't some role-playing girlfriend shit and I'm not paying your slut ass a damn penny."

He pushed me down onto the floor and snatched his belt out of the loops. "Come here!" He grabbed my arms and tied them with his belt. He sat me up on my knees and pried my mouth open with his hands. "You bite me and I swear I will kill you right here, right now." He jammed his penis into my mouth and I couldn't tell what was making me cry louder, the pain from him, or the disappointment in myself. I could see that he was yanking off my clothes and forcing himself into my body, but I had gone numb. Mentally, physically, emotionally, spiritually… I had gone numb.

My best guess of what happened next is that he finished what he was doing and roughed me up a little bit to ensure my silence. When I finally came to, I was in a hospital bed with a tube in my mouth. Everything hurt. There was a nurse in the room checking my chart and when she realized that I was awake, she left the room. A few moments later, a cop walked through the door.

"Nice to see that you're awake. Do you think that you could tell me what happened?" He had kind eyes. They were soft and looked sincere, kind. I told him that I couldn't remember anything and how I was hoping that he could fill in the blanks. "I can only tell you what happened after the manager in the hotel called 911. The officers brought you to the hospital, barely breathing and unconscious, but alive. You were worked over pretty good. The doctors completed a few tests just to get a full view to the extent of your injuries. You have vaginal bruising and bruises on your inner thighs. The bad news is I am sure that whoever attacked you, raped you but the good news is that your baby seems to be healthy."

I was expecting to hear that he could tell that I was raped; I prepared myself for it when I started working, but my heart stopped when he mentioned a baby. What baby?

I was still using and had been off my meds for months now; I was killing my baby and didn't even know it. I couldn't hold back the tears any longer and screamed out in pure agony. I started to rub my stomach and apologize. If I had known that I was pregnant, I would not still be doing the things that I was doing. I promised myself that I would not bring my child into the world cursed with the trifecta like my mother did to me. Now I was just like her.

After I had calmed down a little, I asked to see the doctor for more information. The doctor went over what the cop had just told me. He then added, "In the other tests that I ran I found the existence of heroin in your blood as well as HIV. Did you know that you were positive?" Too disappointed in myself to look at him, I nodded yes. "Ok. Well more good news is that we caught your pregnancy early. You will need to stay here to detox, which won't be easy, and I can start you on the correct medication to fight your HIV from spreading to your child."

I was in the hospital for seven months and had memorized the nurses' schedules. The food tasted like cardboard and at that point I would have probably killed for another channel option. For seven months, I laid in that bed and no one came to visit. Not my mother, not any of my friends…not anyone at all. Being sober allowed me to feel every bit of loneliness of that hospital room. I would get to the point where I wanted to just get up and walk out of that door, but then my baby would kick as if to say, chill mommy, I still got some growing to do. So, I stayed.

I gave birth to my son and he was absolutely beautiful. Seven pounds and eight ounces of pure perfection. The doctor ran a few tests and everything came back great. No HIV, no heroin. He was healthy and we could finally leave the hospital. I gathered all of our things and walked out of the hospital and into a world of unknowns.

I had never had a real job and no one was going to pay for damaged goods. I found a shelter for women and children; they helped me find a job and babysat while I worked. Two years had gone by and things were looking great. I had saved enough money to move out of the shelter and my baby and I were fine. We were fine…but you know that saying that your past always catches up to you; yeah, well, it's true.

I was working one night and an old friend spotted me. He hugged me and looked me up and down. "Hmm still pretty as ever, you wanna taste of the good stuff?" He raised his hand out of his pocket and presented me with an all too familiar baggie. I moved his hand away and told him that I wasn't into that anymore. He just chuckled. "That's what they all say." He put the bag into my bra, "but when you're born into it, you'll never not be into it." And with that, he turned and walked out of the store. I should have yanked it out of my bra and threw it in the trash, but I didn't.

After work I stopped by my neighbor's house to pick my son up and we headed home. Honestly, I had forgotten all about the baggie in my bra and conducted my life as usual. When we got home, I fed my son, we played for awhile, I gave him a bath, and then put him to bed before jumping in the shower myself. I put on my pajamas and headed to bed.

My son usually wakes me up by coming into my room, but the next morning the apartment was silent. I was excited at the idea that he could finally sleep through the night, but now it was time for us to get up and get our day started. As I was walking towards his door, this depressing feeling came over me…something was wrong. I ran into his room and checked to make sure he was in his bed; he was. I released a sigh of relief and proceeded to pack his bag for today. He never slept this long but I figured he was worn out so I waited until I was done, to go wake him up. I whispered, it's time to get up baby. He didn't move. Not even a wiggle. I moved the blanket off of him to pick him up and that's when I saw it. That baggie that I had forgotten all about had somehow ended up in his bed. That baggie that was once full of my past mistakes was now in my son's bed and it was empty.

Cold. My perfectly healthy little boy was now cold as ice. Once I found out that I was pregnant I did everything right, EVERYTHING RIGHT! I was going to prove that I could be a better mother to my child and I couldn't even manage to keep him alive. I couldn't bury my baby, so I just left. I left and never turned back.

Hop forward five years and now I'm here.

Chapter Fourteen - Part Three

I could see her eyes well up with tears as she told us her story, but instead of letting it out she shook her head and took a few deep breaths. Afterwards, it was almost like she did not just say what she had. Tori had clearly learned to fight any emotions that she had.

"So you see doc, you don't know me. You have no idea who I am. Even with me telling you my story you have no idea of who I am. You're probably just sitting back surprised that I haven't killed myself yet, and honestly, I am too. You're probably thinking that I am such a strong woman for making it through but that isn't true either. I'm not strong. Every day I am one disappointment away from swallowing a bottle of pills, but instead I put on a happy and somewhat rude face and crawl through the hours. You said that I'm afraid of letting people in and you're right. If I let people in then they can move closer. If they move closer they can see the edges of the mask I wear. So you all can think I'm some bitch who keeps everyone at bay because it's a lot easier to admit that I'm so damaged internally that I cannot function just being who I really am."

"Wow Tori!"

"Wow! Yeah Lauren, there's my secret. There's what you guys have been asking for."

"Tori your built-up aggression has seemed to…"

"Please don't pull the psych card on me doc. I've been managing without one and I can continue to do so. There is no 'woe is me' sign on my forehead begging for you to fix me."

"I understand, and I will not push it today. But you have been hearing everyone else tell their stories and cry in here, why maintain the façade?"

"Because people think that I am strong. People think that I am strong and people don't ask strong people if they are ok. The less people ask if I am ok, the less I have to lie and say that I am. The less I have to lie about it, the easier it is to keep the mask in place."

"Do you at least feel better telling your story?"

"I'm not sure yet, but some secrets are just not meant to be kept; others will eat at you until you are a figment of your own imagination."

I could not help but think about the secret that was eating at me. How was it that I was able to admit to them that my husband is gay and our marriage is just some business arrangement, but I could not tell them that I was in love with someone else? Why is it that having a gay husband seems so much better than loving a homeless man? He is not technically my patient, so ethically it was fine, but I am a millionaire; I am a princess and the princess only keeps the frog after he turns into a prince. James was no prince. Not in the traditional sense anyway.

"So what now doc? Everyone has officially told you their truth, so what is the rich, great doctor supposed to do now?"

"Well, for starters Tori I am going to…"

"Wait."

I had become so used to Tori being the one that interrupted me that it was strange to hear another voice do it.

"Yes Lauren?"

She looked scared out of her mind. Her palms were beginning to sweat and she could not hold them steady on her wheelchair.

"I lied."

Everyone in the room turned to look at her, which did not help her sweating.

"What did you lie about Lauren?"

"Everything."

"What do you mean everything?"

"I mean everything. I didn't end up in this wheelchair because someone attacked me. The only contest I could ever possibly win is an eating contest. My mother loves me and would never abandon me at a gas station, and…and."

"And what Lauren?"

"And I am not homeless."

The room uproared with questions and quickly became a hostile and uncontrollable environment. As I attempted to regain some type of order, there was a knock on the door. Lily walked in.

"Not right now Lily."

"Dr. Thomas, this isn't a social visit. I need you to come to the lobby."

"Whatever it is, it can wait Lily. Can you not see that I am a little busy at the moment?"

"I understand that, but your husband is asking for you."

My husband was at the front and he was asking for me? My husband? He never just pops up on me anywhere. I knew that it had to be something serious for him to come all of the way down here. Every inch of my body wanted to stay to hear Lauren's explanation of why she would lie about everything but I had to go.

I gathered my things and walked to the lobby; every step dropping my heart lower and lower into my chest. Why was Sebastian here? Had he been fired? Maybe Tony had broken up with him. I smiled at the thought of my husband's boyfriend breaking up with him and him running to me for a shoulder to cry on. How strange that would be.

"Sebastian what is it?"

"Hey Tay. This is a conversation better had in private."

Private. Private conversations always meant that the news would be bad. I was not in the mood for bad news, not with the news that Lauren just shared or Tori's story. I could not handle bad right now. "I…I do not want to talk in private."

"I think it's for the best if we do."

"Sebastian tell me. Just tell me what it is."

Sebastian let out a deep sigh. "It's your dad Tay. He's gone."

"Gone like went on a spontaneous vacation? He likes to do that."

“No Tay. Gone like a car hit him while he was walking to his car. He died on the scene.”

“No. No. That cannot be true. I hit a guy that lived on the streets; he had no one that cared about him. People that have people that care about them do not die in car accidents!”

“We need to go Tay.”

“No. He is not supposed to be dead! He has people that care about him and he died on the street alone like some abandoned dog!”

Sebastian walked over and gave me the tightest hug I had ever had as if he were trying to hold all of my pieces together to keep them from falling, but I couldn’t help it. My father was dead and my body could not take it. My knees buckled and everything inside of me turned cold. Nothing else in the world mattered because the only thing on my mind now was the fact that I did not get to say goodbye.

Chapter Fifteen

The funeral service was lovely. My father was not a weekly church going man, but sacrifices had to be made for him to get where he was in life. He was born into an empty world, but left a legacy of wealth and power behind. I tried to rationalize his death, but the only thing that I could think about was what was going to happen to the person that ran him over. What was going to happen to the murderer who stole my father from me?

I constantly questioned the police, but they would tell me the same thing every time, "We are sorry for your loss ma'am but at this time we have no leads on your father's death."

Murder, not death. Someone had murdered the most influential man I knew and they were going to get away with it while I had to donate millions to charity and got stuck with society's throwaways for a year. Where was the justice in that? I could not make myself understand why the life of some lazy bum was valued higher than the life of my father.

He was killed on his way back from vacation; a vacation that I was supposed to go on. But oh no, I had to stay here and babysit adults that cannot find the intelligence within themselves to get a job and save money so they can live without the help of others. The incompetence level in that building is only immeasurable and I cannot believe that I even thought for a second that they were actual human beings. They are burdens of the state; every last one of them. And now they are personal burdens of mine. I accidentally, permanently harm one of them and get a year sentence of being surrounded by them. But someone murdered my father and they go unpunished. In what world is that even remotely ok?

The judge allowed me to take off a few days off to mourn with my family and bury my father, but those days were up and I am back to the shelter tomorrow. I fear that when I look at them, I will only see injustice. When I look at them I fear that I will feel inadequate because they were able to get justice for one of theirs, but I might never get to confront my father's murderer. When I look at them I fear I will see through them to the other side as though they are not there or look at them the way that I used to. There is no more time to speculate because tomorrow was on its way and it is time to face my fears.

Chapter Sixteen

Walking into the building sent a familiar chill down my spine. I have been volunteering for over a month, but it felt like the first day all over again. I walked into the building angry and hurt, but I held my head high because in no way would they believe that I was weak. In no way would they consider me their equal now that my father was dead.

Lily was at the front desk filing some papers when I walked in. She still had this look of optimism and humbleness; nothing had changed in her world. I kissed my dead father's cheek a week ago, and she was still living her carefree save the weak life. Seeing her joyful immediately pissed me off and sent me spiraling into a dark place.

"Good morning Dr. Thomas. I just wanted to offer my condolences once again and say that I am happy to have you back."

"You can keep your condolences and if losing my father was not hell enough, I am still being forced to come to this waste of space for eleven more months."

"I am sorry that you feel that way Dr. Thomas."

"The once optimistic spark in her eyes had transformed into disappointment."

"What are you looking at Ms. Green?"

"Pain. People all grieve in their own ways and I can see past the mask you spent hours applying before getting in the car and coming here."

"I am done grieving for your information. It is not grief that you see on my face, it is the eye-opening realization that these infestations that you choose to waste your time on, will always somehow beat the system. They can eat with no job, go to the doctor with no healthcare and live a full life with no money until the day they die; even in death they are treated like royalty. You are merely a pawn to be used in their abuse of the system, and one day you will wake up and realize the same thing. One day you will wake up and realize that if it is you against them, they will always win; they will always have more people on their side."

Lily sighed and shook her head as though she was ridding herself of every last thing that I said. I will be waiting for the day that the truth is revealed to her just as it was revealed to me.

"I'm sorry that you feel that way Dr. Thomas. I must admit I had hopes that being here and hearing their stories would humanize them to you. I pray that it still does."

"Keep your prayers… no one is listening."

I turned my back to Lily and headed down the hall to the session room. In attempts to somewhat calm myself down I walked slower than usual. It did not help. By the time my fingertips were on the door, my blood was boiling and I wanted nothing more than to go in there, tell them how I feel and walk away, but that was not an option that I had. Their community of speed bumps had stolen that from me.

"Hey doc you're back!"

James was the first to notice me walk through the door; he was always the first to notice me. I instantly had flashbacks of our talks and the sex, but I buried them because behind all of that he was still one of them. I could not allow myself to be with one of them.

"Everyone sit down so we can get started." No one listened. They were too busy crowded around one of the tables in the back to notice that I had come into the room.

"EVERYONE SIT DOWN!!"

Everyone whipped their necks to the door to see who was screaming. Once they realized that it was me standing at the door, they began to offer their generic "I'm sorry" and "I'm praying for you." Every word that left their mouth, left my ear just as quick. I did not come back to this place to talk or hear them fake care. I was only back here for one reason, my father wanted me to finish my sentence and move on to have babies. My plan was to stick with his plan.

"Well someone needs some sex."

"What did you just say to me Tori?"

"I thought I was speaking clearly, my apologies. I said that someone needs some sex, insinuating that maybe if your gay husband would throw you a bone every now and then you could replace that pole up your ass with something more fun."

"You are way out of line Tori! No, no I retract that statement. You are out of line for a sane, functioning adult but you are right in line with the lazy, idiotic, inferior beings that lurk in this very room and disease society."

"Wow! I was only joking, but it is nice to see the real you reveal itself once again instead of the fake, 'I care' mask you have been trying to hold into place lately. You used all of us to get what you needed and I can only be mad at myself. I knew the type of person you were, but I decided to fight my gut. I decided to let you in. Thank you for showing me that I… no that we all made a mistake."

"You all made a mistake? You believe that you all made a mistake in judging my character? Well that is great, because I know now that I did not make a mistake judging you all. You people are all the same."

Tori looked around the room as her face becomes even more confused. "We aren't the same race, gender or even the same age. What do you mean by "you people?"

"You people. The poors! The homeless and the hopeless! The vain of my very existence! And the only thing that keeps me sane is the fact that a year from now, this will all be a bad dream; a year from now I will be going on the vacation that I was supposed to go on with my father and I will be there alone. It is only fair, because I was the reason that he had to go alone this year. No, actually, you all were the reason that he had to go alone this year. You all and your pathetic lives provided the need for such a punishment. I did not spend most of my life in school to work with charity cases and I definitely did not spend the time to create a source of a consequence; a consequence for something that would never have happened if you all and your entire homeless community were not so lazy and unmotivated to make something of yourselves AND GET OFF OF THE STREETS!!"

"Did you bump your head and forget everything that we shared with you?"

"No Francesca. I did not bump my head; I wish this was something that could be cured by an aspirin."

"You guys, she didn't bump her head. Don't you see what has happened?"

Garrett looks at the group amazed that no one can answer his question and they looked back at him in preparation for him to continue. They could not even understand each other. How did I ever believe that they would be able to understand me. Their mental capacities were far too minuscule to understand.

"Will you just tell us what you are getting at Garrett?"

Naomi had clearly become impatient waiting for Garrett.

"Ok ok. You guys remember the last time we were in a session and the doc got pulled out because her husband was at the door?"

"Yeah the butt pirate."

"Not cool, Tori."

"Sorry Craig. Well at least you are out with your penile to penile desires."

"It's hard to come out of the closet."

"Yeah, the whole trying to cut your penis off and having your dad disown and abuse you for being gay kind of proved that it's hard to come out of the closet. I was in the room too when you told your story."

"Well then act like it Tori. Act like you have some type of understanding of how hard it is."

"What does any of this have to do with why doc is over here spazzing?"

"I was getting there Lauren."

Seeing Lauren when I walked into the room today almost made me forget about my problems, because I was so interested in why someone would lie and say that they were homeless. Who in their right mind would do that?

"Oh, now we are supposed to listen to a liar?"

"Tori, will you shut up about that already? Maybe if you were this focused on your own child you wouldn't be here right now."

"What the hell did you just say to me!?"

"Look, I just want to know what Garrett was going to say about the doc and you guys refuse to let him finish."

"Oh, he can finish, but it's going to have to be after you fess up. You want to judge me. I admitted to my flaws no matter how ugly they are. I am not the one wheeling around in a homeless shelter during the night and living a completely different life when she wakes up in the morning. Are you even handicapped or was that a lie to?!"

Tori hopped out of her seat and ran to Lauren. She got to the side of her chair and pushed it over.

The chair hit the ground so hard that it knocked over a nearby plant. Lauren just laid there. I wondered how long she would stay on the ground like that before she got up and walked out of this room.

"Was that a lie too Lauren? Huh? Huh? At least if I did still have my child, I would not have raised him to be a damn liar."

The entire room stood frozen; waiting to see if Lauren could actually walk. A few moments passed and when she did not get up, Francesca ran to help her up.

"What does it matter if she lied about how she got here? The only thing that matters is that she is here and that makes her family."

"No Frannie you are wrong! She does not belong here; she is no family of mine."

"Well technically…"

"Technically what Lauren?"

The topic of my attitude had been swept under the rug as everyone waited on the edge of their seats in disbelief and curiosity. If Lauren was not truly homeless then why had she lied about it? She could have easily come as a volunteer and helped around the shelter, but she wanted to be homeless. Whatever accident that she was in, must have affected her brain as well.

"Well Lauren, we are all waiting."

Tori was in no mood for Lauren's vague answers today.

"Fine, Tori just shut up! Shut the hell up! I will tell you guys my story…my real story."

LAUREN

I didn't grow up on the streets; to be honest I barely walked on them. My father is a minister for one of the biggest churches on this coast and my mother is a World Religions professor for an ivy league school. Needless to say, I am far…far from being homeless.

My parents were pretty busy most days but they still wanted to have their values and morals instilled in me, so they made sure that I grew up in the church. While they were at work, I would be in bible study or choir rehearsal or praise dance practice. I wasn't lying about my ability to put on a show; I just put the spotlight on a different stage. Honestly, every aspect of my life was under a spotlight.

I am an only child and that proved to be a blessing and a curse. My parents would give me anything that I asked for: cars, clothes, trips, shoes; but it all came with stipulations. I can have a car but I had a 10 o'clock curfew. I had an unlimited fund to buy clothes, but they had to be approved by my parents first. Any trips had to have a religious aspect to them, and my heels weren't allowed to be over 4 inches. They said that they had these rules to protect me from the evils of the world, but honestly, they just pissed me off. I wanted to see the evils of the world so that I could judge them for myself. I wanted to taste temptation and see if it was as sweet as everyone said that it was. I got that chance about two years ago.

It started off as a normal service; the seats filled as the choir sang. Their tune was so intoxicating that it brought every sinner in to fellowship and cleanse their souls; even if only for one day.

As the congregation settled, my father made his way to the mic. That was usually the time that he gave the Morning Prayer, but instead he told us that he had a surprise. He looked to his left, and when he moved he revealed this angel of a man. He had smooth skin and broad shoulders. Just by looking at him you could tell that he had a testimony that he had been through trials and tribulations, but his eyes remained pure and joyous.

My father needed more help in the church so he hired a new deacon. He didn't even hold official interviews because the man that he hired was a former student of my mothers and she gave him a glowing recommendation. My father may have put God first in his life, but my mother was a close second. The love and respect that they have for each other was inspiring to grow up around. I could listen to the story of how they met in church over and over again; just imagining when I would meet "the one" on a cool Sunday morning. We would lock eyes as we walked up for communion and at that moment it would be undeniably clear that God had put us in the same room, at the same time just so we could fall in love. I went to church happily knowing that it was the place where I would find my soul mate lurking in the pews. Not once did I suspect that I would have to look up from one of the pews to find him.

My father introduced him to the entire church family, but I could only focus on the slight moment when our eyes met as he scanned the room. It was the moment that I had been dreaming about my entire life. My thoughts immediately switched from the sermon of the day to planning our future together. He could take over the church when my father retired and after I graduated high school, I could go on to college and become a professor just like my mother. Personally, I want more than one child because I know how hard it was for me to make friends growing up and I wanted my children to always have friends; always have someone to talk to when they needed help. I questioned who his groomsmen would be at the wedding and how he would tear up as I walked down the aisle. It was all so perfect.

The church service was to welcome him into our minds and welcome him into our hearts. My mother always cooked Sunday dinner and my parents would invite different people over sometimes. Tonight, they decided to invite the new deacon over to give him a warm welcome. I wanted to give him a warm welcome of my own. The way I felt when I looked at him was nothing I'd ever experienced before. I knew that it would be inappropriate to express my feelings for him in my parents' home, so I planned to just avoid him entirely until dinner was ready.

As my mother was cooking, my father and the new deacon sat in his study having a pre-dinner scotch. My parents would have a drink or two when company came, but I have yet to see them drunk. My father would tell me, "When you are old enough one drink is ok, but always remember Luke 21:34 - Drunkenness will cause a person not to be ready for the Lord's return." To drink was acceptable to them on occasions, but to be drunk was a clear sin and abomination. After their drink, they began trading stories. I just so happened to walk by as my mother called for my father's help in the kitchen. "Excuse me young man," he said to the deacon, "duty calls." "Lauren come in. How about you give him a tour of the house while I help your mother?" My heart jumped into my throat. I hesitantly agreed and as my father headed to the kitchen, I took the new deacon around the house.

I hadn't been that close to him before then, but now I could tell that he even smelled heavenly. I know that lust is a sin, but everything about him screamed my gift from God himself. I didn't even care that he was seven years older than me; my parents are six years apart themselves, so another year didn't mean much. I don't know what came over me, but somewhere in between showing him the den and the library, I couldn't control myself. I kissed him.

Quickly, I pulled away and apologized while calling myself stupid. He just stared at me…not saying a word. I turned around to go clean the embarrassment off of my face, but he caught my wrist and spun me around. He kissed me back and the world I knew was gone; in its place now lay something far more beautiful. We both knew that this was wrong morally and highly disrespectful but we couldn't help ourselves. "Dinner is ready!" My mother's voice snapped us out of our trance and back to reality. This could not happen; not here, not now.

Dinner was a bit awkward, but my parents didn't seem to notice. They carried on conversation as usual, never noticing the pink elephant in the room. We finished eating and after about two hours, the ordeal was all over. My father walked the deacon to the door and they shook hands. He glanced back, and I knew that the unfinished feeling that was eating at my stomach was chopping on his as well. What I didn't know was when we would have the opportunity to finish what we started.

A few weeks passed, and it seemed like our moment would never come. We would exchange secret glances of pure passion, but it didn't go any further than that. I had given up on us ever having our moment, but then the greatest thing happened; my choir director got really sick. It wasn't great that she got sick; the magical part about her pain was that someone had to step up and take her place while she healed. That person just so happened to be the deacon. Practice went as planned and after it was over, I stayed back to help clean up. Time alone with him seemed to fly by. Seconds felt like hours, and with neither of us talking, it was unbearable. I was stacking the chairs when he called me over to him. He stared into my eyes, into my soul and he asked, “Are you sure about this?” I reassured him that I was more than sure. He was my soul mate and if God had created him just for Him and me, then why should we wait. We made love right there on the practice room floor and it was everything I imagined and more.

I wanted to give him my number so that we could talk outside of church, but my parents checked the phone records. It was no telling what they would do if they were to find out. We would have to be satisfied with our stolen glances and contain our love making to the practice room. This went on for months and everything was perfect but you know that old saying; ‘what’s done in the dark comes to the light,’ and I was about to find out just how true that was. 1Corinthians 6:18 Flee from sexual immorality. Every other sin a person commits is outside the body, but the sexually immoral person sins against his own body.

I was three weeks late and after I took a few dozen home tests my fears were confirmed. I was pregnant. I was a junior in high school, far off from being a wife. So how was I supposed to birth a bastard baby? The only comfort that I found in the situation was that I knew who the father of my child was and I knew that he would be there for me. I would have to wait until the next practice to tell him, but I knew that he would be excited and that he would know what to do next.

The room cleared after practice and he ran to pick me up and put me onto the piano. As he was unbuttoning his pants and kissing my neck, I figured there was no time like the present. I whispered in his ear that I was pregnant. His entire body froze. I was sure that I even felt his heart completely stop for a few seconds. "What did you just say?" His usual calm, joyous tone had been replaced with a harsh, angry one. I repeated that I was pregnant and he stepped back and buttoned his pants back up. "We can't do this." I told him that I was sure that we could still have sex during the pregnancy. "I'm not talking about the sex Lauren. We can't do THIS." He grabbed his jacket and walked out of the room. It was so not the reaction that I expected.

Part of me thought that he was going to leave me alone to have this child and the thought was unbearable. After that night, I locked myself in my bedroom and refused to come out. I told my parents that I was focused on studying for my SATs so they didn't bother me much; only to tell me to come to dinner or tell me how proud they were of me. A piece of me died every time that they said they were proud of me. If they knew the truth, it would break their hearts. "Lauren come downstairs. You have a visitor." Who could it be, I wondered. I walked to the living room only to be greeted by the deacon. "Alright sweetheart, I have a meeting to get to so I will see you later. Deacon if you can please stay for dinner, it was such a pleasure to have you the last time." And with that my mother disappeared outside, leaving the deacon and I to deal with the growing pink elephant in the room ourselves.

He pulled an envelope out of his jacket and pointed it in my direction with, "this is for you." I'm not sure what I thought it would be, but when I opened it, I was surprised. It was a stack of twenty dollar bills. He must have noticed the confusion on my face, because he went on to explain what the money was for. "Look Lauren we can't do this. We are not married. I am a twenty-three year old deacon and you are still a kid. You cannot do this. Now I am not sure how much these things cost, but if you need more just let me know." He said it like we were buying a Christmas gift. I screamed, "SAY IT! If this is what he wanted then he would have to look me in the eyes and directly ask for it." "Get an abortion Lauren." I cried that this was our baby and that we could make it work. "There is no way Lauren, not now…not ever. Get the abortion and take care of yourself kid." And with that he kissed me on the forehead and walked out the door. How could he be so cruel? How could I be so stupid? I grabbed my keys and left the house, slamming the door on my way out.

If he wanted me to get an abortion then that is exactly what I would do. I tried not to think about it but while waiting at a red light I caught a glance of a woman pushing her baby in a stroller up the street with her husband right by her side. Why was she able to have it all and I was cursed with a baby conceived out of wedlock and a man who just wants me to get rid of it like spoiled milk. I broke into tears and laid my head on the steering wheel. When I hit the steering wheel, the horn blew and my first thought was that it was someone behind me telling me that it was our turn to go so I went. It wasn't our turn…

They told me that when I ran the red light an 18-wheeler was driving through the intersection and he clipped me. The car flipped a few times and my legs were stuck between the car for a few hours until they could get the Jaws of Life and get me out. "You are lucky to be alive." If I survived the crash maybe God did love me. I tried to lift up and properly thank the doctor but I couldn't. "As I said before, you are lucky to be alive Lauren. You lost a lot of blood and needed a blood transfusion and the pressure of the car proved to be too much stress on your legs. I am sorry to tell you this but we could not restore mobility, you will never walk again. I am also sorry to tell you that we could not save the baby either." Oh, how I wish my parents weren't in the room right now. I assumed that they would lecture me and throw bible verses at my head while drowning me in holy water but they just walked out of the room. I would have preferred them to scream, because then at least I would know how they felt.

"This is all our fault." I woke up to the sound of my mother's voice. She and my father were having what sounded like a fight. I had never seen them fight; they probably just thought that I was still sleep. "This is our fault. We have kept this secret from her and now she had a secret that she kept from us. She is going to find out. She needed blood and we could not give it to her. She is going to find out the truth and hate us because it almost cost her life."

My curiosity had reached an overflow and I had to know what they were talking about so I called them into my room. I asked them to just tell me whatever they have been keeping from me; just tell me. They were both silent. It quickly became exhausting to just hear them breathe, so I yelled at them to just tell me. "Ren," my mother only called me that when the next thing out of her mouth was going to be something that made me mad, "Ren, baby you have to understand. We only kept this from you to protect you." She got silent again and started to tear up. "Lauren what your mother is trying to say is that you lost a lot of blood in the accident, you almost died. You almost died and there was nothing we could do. There was nothing that we could do because you needed blood and we couldn't give you any." He released a long deep sigh. "We couldn't give you any blood because we don't have the same blood because biologically…we are not your parents. We adopted you after you were abandoned by your birth mother."

A million and one questions flashed in my head, but I could only get one of them to come out, "what happened?" They handed me a piece of paper and told me that if I wanted to find my birth parents, that they would do everything they could. I wanted to, so they hired a private investigator for me and we got started.

Chapter Sixteen - Part Two

"That still doesn't explain why you are here playing homeless especially when you are filthy rich."

Lauren took out a piece of paper from her jacket. "This is why I am here."

She started to read from it. I am happy that her secret would be out soon so we could get back to focusing on me and my problem.

"For whomever may be reading. My name is Mariah Alexander. I was born on March 5, 1999 and I have type AB blood. I am allergic to bananas and mangos. In the bag is my favorite blanket and an envelope with all the money I have to my name. As her mother, I can no longer take care of her the way that she deserves and it is my deepest and most sincere prayer that someone who can finds her. Please take care of her and let her know that I love her and will always love her. Everything that I do is for her protection."

"So, you found out that your birth mother loved you too? I am still not seeing what the hell that has to do with you coming here to laugh in our face. What does that have to do with anything at all? You expect us to feel sorry for you because of this? You expect us to…"

"Shut up Tori! Just shut the hell up for one damn second!"

Nash

I am not sure what had gotten into Francesca, but I knew that she knew something that we did not. The look in her eyes was a combination of fear and excitement.

"Could, umm, could I see that letter?"

Lauren hesitantly gave the letter to Francesca. Francesca stared at the paper with such intensity that I was waiting for her to burn a hole into it. Then she just started to bawl uncontrollably.

"What is wrong with you Frannie?!"

"Do you know what this means Tori? It's me. I'm the reason that she's here. She, she, she's my daughter."

Every single jaw in the room dropped to the floor. We were all thinking that Lauren was just some coward hanging around homeless people to somehow feel better about herself, but in reality, she just wanted to find her birth mother; the woman that left her in a hospital.

Again, they had managed to make everything about them. No one cared about what I was going through anymore, just because a mother and daughter were reunited. I did not have to be reunited with my father; I was able to know him my entire life just for him to be stolen from me. It did not matter to me that they missed out on sixteen years together because they had each other now. They continued to win and celebrate, while my father's killer still roamed the streets a free man.

"Ok, so she is your daughter and she took the time to find you, are we all caught up here?"

"Woah there doc, you must still be hurting from that accident."

"And what accident might you be referring to Naomi?"

“The one that’s got a pole stuck where the sun don’t shine.”

“Oh, that is so clever. Did you steal that joke or did one of your many, many cell mates tell it to you?”

“Hey that’s uncalled for!”

“Oh, great now the “queen” is going to try to tell me how I should talk to people.”

“Really doc? What did Naomi or Craig or any of us do to you?”

“You want to know what you all did Garrett. You guys stole the time away from me that I could have been spending with my father. You guys are the reason that I missed our vacation and you guys are the reason that he died ALONE! He was murdered and I had to bury him without getting him the justice that he deserves. The human sewage rat that I hit by accident was able to get justice, but my father, a man who actually made good use of his life might not ever get justice. I do not care about your PTSD or the fact that Lauren lied to be close to Francesca. I do not care about any of you or your problems!!!”

“Oh. So now you don’t care about any of us? Not a single one?”

James had been completely silent today; I had actually forgotten that he was even in the room. Part of me wanted to scream out how much I did care for him; proclaim my love. The other part of me knew that in reality we would never be able to be together. He would always be one of them and I would always be me. Our worlds crash and burn when they collide and no good would come out of us.

“No James. Not a single one.” I could not tell if the shattering sound that came after the sentence left my tongue, came from his heart or mine.

Chapter Seventeen

"Just read the damn thing Tay."

The caring, thoughtful husband act had faded and the true Sebastian had returned. He started sleeping at home again and I could see traces of Tony around the house. Every sock or extra toothbrush made me sick to my stomach. The reality was that my husband would never truly be my husband. I had been spending so much time with James, that I had almost forgotten what it meant to be alone. The haunting silence that made room for every degrading, hopeless thought that came across my mind was back. The fact that I had fallen in love with James just to toss him away, did not help either. There was no way he would forgive me for my outburst at the shelter. If I was him, I would not forgive someone like me either. Someone like me, did not deserve forgiveness from anyone. The voices that lurked in the silence had proven that.

"It is my letter Sebastian, and I will read it whenever I decide to."

"Don't be stupid. The funeral was weeks ago and you still refuse to read his will. Whatever it is that he left for you needs to be claimed, so that they can figure out what to do with the remainder of his assets."

"I will not rush into reading it, just so a bunch of savages can rip into my father's life savings. I have everything that I need."

"Why must you be so stubborn?"

"Well I hear that lack of sex turns you into a real bitch, so maybe that is my problem."

"You should go out and have sex then."

"Well most married women like to have sex with their husbands."

"Well most husbands don't marry their wives just to be a walking, talking wallet."

"Well most wives do not marry their husbands and expect to be replaced by his male employee in the bedroom!"

"Don't play the victim card here. You knew exactly the type of life I lived when you married me. I never kept that part of my life from you, but you decided to ignore it so that you could continue to live the lifestyle that you were accustomed to. It's not like I sold you this dream that we would be happily married and start a family, you knew walking in that this was a business move and nothing more. You chose this life, so don't paint me as the bad guy when all of a sudden it isn't working for you anymore. No one is forcing you to be here. You can leave whenever the hell you want to, just make sure you leave my keys and cards on the table when you walk out. You have nothing without me, so you forfeit the option to have an opinion on the way I live my life. I hate to sound generic, but get with it, or get lost."

I was nothing but a mask to him. He would come and put me on when he wanted to fool the world, but as soon as Halloween was over, he would toss me to the back of the closet. He had no problem using me as a cloak, and there was a time when I had no problem using him as a bank, but now I wanted more. Now that

I have tasted being with someone who cares about the person that I am on the inside, I wanted Sebastian to become this person. But he was right. I knew the deal going in and I knew the type of man that I married. I just never knew that I would be tempted with intimacy. Beyond the amazing sex that we shared, James and I had this energy that connects when we are around each other and overtakes any room. People could feel the aura, but no one could tell that it came from our secret love. As long as no one could tell, we could have continued to live the happy life that we were, but I just had to go crazy on the entire group. It has been a few days of the silent treatment again and it is starting to drive me crazy…again.

Chapter Eighteen

"Hello everyone, such a lovely day to talk."

No one responded.

"Or you all could continue to be childish and not talk to me at all."

Still silence.

"Looks like you guys are going to keep this up. It's fine. You want silence? I can be silent for the next ten months too. No problem."

They just sat there; they would not even look at me. Things had progressed beyond the silent treatment now; it was like I was not even in the room. Garrett, Francesca, Craig, not even Tori, would acknowledge that I was in the room. Everyone was doing something, anything to avoid my presence. The worst part about it was that since I blew up that day, James has not come back to the shelter. I have been having nightmares of someone hitting him with their car because they failed to see him sleeping on the side of the road. They would be like me, assume that he did not have anyone who loved him and rule his death as an accident. Spilling milk is an accident, locking your keys in the car is an accident, but for someone to hurt James would not be an accident…it would be a tragedy. I just buried my father; I was not in the mental state to bury someone else that I loved. No matter how wrong it may be, James is indeed someone that I love. I have to find him and fix things before it is too late. He does not deserve to die thinking that he was in the world alone; I just need to figure out where he is.

"Has anyone seen James?"

Silence.

"Has anyone talked to him?"

Silence.

"Look! I understand that you all do not want to talk to me and that is fine, I get it, but right now I need to know where he is!"

Silence.

"Yeah that works too I guess. You are all going to play the silent game again. I am

beyond tired of this game."

"Damn it! You just don't get it do you?! This isn't a game, this was never a game! You come in here with your expectations of who we are already embedded in your head. You walk around in your eight hundred dollar pumps, after getting out of your one hundred-thousand-dollar car and expect us to believe that you ever cared. It was never a secret that you were forced to be here, you've heard our stories…SO WERE WE! You turn your head up at us, but honestly you are the coward. So, you can hide behind your diamonds or your beach homes, but I am the one that sees you. I was you! So focused on maintaining this image that you were ready and willing to sell your soul and now when you wake up in the morning you can barely recognize who the fuck you are!

You can't even admit what you really want to yourself, so you are fine with living an unhappy life with a gay husband. I see you doc! I was you!!"

Normally I would have told Tori that she had gone overboard and overstepped her boundaries, but she was right. How was I to judge them for their situations, when mine were far from perfect? The money would always be there; it had always been there. It has never been able to cure my loneliness, no matter how many friends would attach themselves to me for what I had and not who I was. I am not sure if I even knew who I was.

"You are absolutely right Tori."

"I'm right? Wait did you just say, that I was right doc? Who are you and what have you done with the demon daughter that usually comes in?"

"You are right, but right now I do not have time to deal with my issues; I just need to find James. Do you know where he is?"

"Oh."

"Oh, what Craig?"

"Oh, I see what this is. You must need all of us to make it through your little therapy jail sentence for your time to even count. You are just using us."

"That is not it."

"Then what is it doc? We would all like to know."

"It is none of your business."

Everyone in the room began to shout, demanding an answer. I tried to ignore them, but they just got louder and louder. I could not keep it in any longer…

“BECAUSE I LOVE HIM! I NEED TO FIND JAMES BECAUSE I LOVE HIM!”

“Whoa!”

“Yeah whoa Lauren. So, if any of you have any idea where he is, could you please tell me?”

“He said that he would be picking up any job that he could in the area so you better start looking.”

Well that was not very insightful, but at least now I knew that he was still in town. I had no idea of where I was going to start but now I had an area.

“Thank you.”

Chapter Nineteen

He must have really wanted to never see my face again if he decided to pick up all of the extra jobs. I always thought that I knew that love looked like diamonds and cars. James did not have any of that, but every time he looked at me, my heart skipped a beat. If he brushed against my shoulder in the shelter, my insides would melt and I would check the floor to make sure nothing seeped through my shoes. To merely be in his presence was the greatest gift I have ever received and every second in his absence, felt like a lifetime. If this was not love, then it is some cruel, cruel joke.

I started looking for him at the places that he had worked before. I would look for the person in charge but they all said the same thing, "He has been working here but not today." Part of me was happy to hear that he was taking a day off, part of me was confused as why a man in his position would think that it was wise to take a day off. All of me just wanted to know that he was ok.

I could not think of anywhere else to look so I decided to head home. Maybe after a good night's rest I would be able to think of more places to look. I only looked down at my phone for a second but in that second I was completely blind to the person walking. Not this again! I could not deal with another year in the shelter because some other delinquent decided to play speed bump in the middle of the night. I slammed on my brakes and after a few moments of silence, I debated on just driving away, but if they were still by my car and I drove over them, it would ruin the paint job.

I turned my car off, but kept the lights on so I could see what was going on. Once I got to the front I immediately wished that I could unsee what was waiting for me. The answers I had been looking for, the search that consumed my night, they were all over. I found James…or rather he found me.

"James! James is that you?! What are you doing out here? I could have killed you just now!"

He was able to stand up but I could tell that something was wrong. The look in his eyes, the one that made me melt as the butterflies swarmed in my abdomen, it was gone. The look that it was replaced by was one that I had never seen before.

"That's her. No it's not, she left you. She doesn't love you. No it has to be her, I mean it looks like her and that's her car. That is her car right? You should know. You are the one that did those things in her car you naughty boy. I'm not naughty, we are in love. In love? No one will ever love you. Why would they, you are a worthless bum."

It was just that quick that I realized what was wrong. James had stopped taking his meds and from this display it seemed like he stopped taking them when he left the shelter. I walked over and wrapped my arms around him.

"James. James! This is not you! The people in your head are lying! You are worthy, I love you. I love you James!"

"You…love…me. But you can't love me. You, you said that. You said that you can't love me, so you can't say that you love me now when you said that you can't love me. You're lying. You're a liar either then or now. You are a liar."

"I know what I said James, but it was only because I was afraid. I was afraid to tell anyone that I had fallen in love with you. But I am not afraid anymore James. I love you and I want to tell the world. I will tell the world; you just have to get better."

"I used to be better. I think I can be better again. Will…will you help me?"

"Oh my God yes! Yes I will help you James. Just get in the car."

"Ok. But can you help me? I don't feel so…"

"James! JAMES! WAKE UP!!"

I did not notice his leg until he passed out. James must have gotten his leg cut by something on my car and the entire time that we were talking he was losing blood.

"Doctor Thomas your patient is out of surgery, you can go see him now."

My patient? Last night I was proclaiming my love to him in the middle of the road and now I had walked into this place and told them that he was my patient. At this point I was just glad that whatever I said when I got here, they granted me visitation. I had to make sure that James was ok.

I walked into the room and his doctor went over his chart. James was still asleep, but as long as he was alive, it was good that he was getting some rest.

"Excuse me, who are you?"

"My apologies doctor, I am Dr. Thomas. James is my, he is my patient."

"Nice to meet you Dr. Thomas, I have good and bad news."

Ok let me hear it.

"The good news is that we were able to stop the bleeding and fix the break. The bad news is that an infection had already set in from a previous injury and he is going to need another surgery to clean it out."

"Ok. I do not understand why you all have not performed the surgery already if that is what he needs."

"His insurance covered fixing his leg and his psych meds, but they do not include the other surgery. We are not allowed to perform any treatment without the patient having proper insurance."

"You cannot be serious right now. You mean to tell me that this infection will continue to spread and eventually kill him and you refuse to treat it before it does?"

"Yes ma'am. It is hospital policy."

"Ok, ok. I have amazing insurance that covers everything from a runny nose to a heart transplant, could you just use mine?"

"Insurance can only be shared with family members and spouses. You are his doctor; you do not fall in either category."

"What if I did?"

"What if you did what?"

"What if I fell into one of those categories? What if we were married? Is there a way to make that happen in here?"

“Well, yes but you would need his consent.”

“I can get that as soon as he wakes up.”

“I will send the minister down whenever you are ready.”

“Thank you.”

“Do not thank me; just be sure that this is what you want to do. We are not talking about you picking up the tab at dinner; you are committing your life to him.”

“I understand completely. I will call you when he wakes up.”

Chapter Twenty

Seconds quickly turned into minutes, minutes escalated into hours. He was not waking up and the beeping of the machines was about to drive me insane. I cannot bare the idea that he would not open his eyes and the fact that it would be because of me, would kill me.

rasped voice doc. Hey doc is that you?

Oh my god he is awake. “Yes. Yes it is me, James.”

“Hi. How are you?”

“I am good. I am really good now. How are you?”

“I’m in a little pain, but I’m ok. The voices are gone again.”

“That is good. They gave you some of your meds and fixed your leg. However I do have some bad news.”

“Hit me with it doc.”

“You have an infection. It is from an old injury and if they do not fix it, it will kill you.”

“Ok. So when are they going to fix it?”

“That is the bad news…they are not going to fix it. Your insurance does not cover it or the surgery.”

“Well that’s just my luck. So how long before it puts me in a grave?”

“It does not have to. I have an idea.”

“I’m up for anything that keeps me kicking.”

“My insurance would cover the surgery. I could let you use it.”

“That is a great plan doc, but insurance doesn’t work like that. We ain’t family, we ain’t married, and they ain’t letting me use your insurance.”

"We could fix that. There is a minister in the hospital. He could perform the ceremony and once we are married I can do the paperwork to add you on my insurance.”

“Shouldn’t you already have your current husband on your insurance?”

“We have separate policies, part of our arrangement. The less we have connecting us on paper the better.”

“It is still very much against the law to be married to more than one person at one time.”

“I will worry about that. Do you want to get married so you can use my insurance or not?”

“No. I don’t want to get married so that I can use your insurance.”

“James you will die without the surgery! Please let me help you.”

“Taylor I don’t want to get married to you so that I can use your insurance…I want to marry you because you saw me at my worst out there after you hit me, and you still decided to be by my side. I know your story, the reason you ended up at the shelter in the first place. You hit somebody just like me and you showed no remorse, you continued to refer to him as a being less than the ground you walked on. You could have easily done the same thing with me, but you didn't. You love me and I love you and that is why I want to marry you. Everything in your life doesn't have to be a business arrangement."

Of course I had heard someone say I love you before but when hearing it from James' mouth, it felt different. It felt forever. There were a thousand words that I wanted to say to him, but nothing seemed powerful enough to explain my love for him. No words could explain my gratitude to him for healing my spirit. "I will call downstairs and have them send the minister up. We can get married and you can be on my insurance within the hour."

"Did you hear anything that I just said?"

"Within the hour James."

Chapter Twenty-One

"Good morning Dr. Thomas."

"Good morning Lily. You look like you are doing better today."

"I am thank you. Is everyone in the room?"

'Yes ma'am"

"I am going to head back, have a nice day."

"Thank you, you do the same."

I had not been back to the shelter since my outburst where I proclaimed my love for James to the group; I knew that they would have even more questions especially since he was back now too. I could only imagine the comments and jokes that would shoot my way as soon as I turned the doorknob. Almost all of me wanted to turn around, run away and never come back to this place, but I could not leave him again. I also did not want to deal with the repercussions of not finishing my year sentence. I doubt that the judge would feel that generous towards me. Sink or swim, there was no more running now. I walked into the room.

"Welcome back doc."

"Hello Lauren, I am surprised to see you here."

"Well I don't live here anymore, but I still come to visit so I can spend time with my mom and the rest of the family."

"How does your actual family feel about you coming here?"

"With all due respect doc, these people are my actual family. If you are referring to my parents, they encouraged me to have a relationship with Frannie once I told them why she gave me up. They raised me to be forgiving of others and understanding of their past. We all have skeletons and I'm no mortician."

"You aren't really in the position to still be judging anyway doc."

"I was wondering how long you could remain quiet Tori. I was not judging her, just asking a simple question. You are right, I am a married millionaire doctor that fell in love with a schizophrenic homeless man…I have no room to judge."

"I am right here doc."

"No offense James."

"I admire you doc. I didn't like you before, but now you are doing something that I wish I had the courage to do."

"Thanks, I guess Craig. What is it that you want the courage to do?"

"Admit to the world who I love."

There was that word again. I felt like a teenager when the word was used. It was still a new experience for me overall. I loved my family, but that was because they are my family and that is what you were supposed to do. To love and be loved by someone on purpose is an entirely different feeling.

"Dr. Thomas, there are some men that want to see you in the lobby."

Well there goes that feeling. The last time that I had an expected guest here it was Sebastian coming to tell me that my father was dead. What bad news could someone be bringing for me today?

"Ok Lily. I will be right back everyone."

During the walk to the lobby I could see that Lily kept tugging her fingers as though she was nervous about something.

"Lily what is it?"

"I don't know Dr. Thomas."

"Well who is in the lobby?"

"They are…"

She pointed to the door where two police officers stood conversing. James did not die from the accident; I actually ended up saving his life. Who knows how long it would have taken them to discover the infection if I did not hit him and put him in the hospital. He was alive and well so the need for officers was baffling to me.

"Are you Dr. Taylor Thomas?"

"Yes."

"Are you also Dr. Taylor Bradley?"

My heart sank to my shoes. I knew that there was a possibility that someone may find out that I got married again, but I never thought that they would figure it out so quickly. I had two options now. I could lie, but then they might go after James for insurance fraud or I could tell the truth and take the punishment. The year of mandatory volunteer work at the shelter was already overwhelming; I could not handle the possibility of serving time behind actual bars. My life needs more than one outfit or scheduled showers.

"Ma'am are you also Dr. Taylor Bradley?"

They were waiting for my answer and had no intention of backing down or leaving before they got one. I had no more time to think it over.

"Yes… yes I am also Dr. Taylor Bradley."

"Are you aware that polygamy is against the law in this state?"

"Yes officer I am."

"Were you aware that you were still married to Mr. Thomas when you married Mr. Bradley?"

"Yes officer I was aware."

"Ma'am we are going to need for you to come with us."

"I understand."

I turned to Lily who was trying her best to avoid listening to our conversation, but failing horribly.

"Lily here are my keys. Will you make sure to inform the group that I will not be returning to our session and find someone to drop my car off to my home?

"Yes of course Dr. Thomas."

"Thank you Lily."

I turned back to the officers. "I am ready."

"Dr. Thomas you are under arrest."

"I know my Miranda rights, you do not have to waste your time."

"Please put your hands behind your back."

"Is this really necessary?"

"Yes ma'am it is. Please put your hands behind your back."

I complied with their request. The cold cuffs on my wrist made me feel like I had just robbed a bank or blew up a school. They screamed criminal when all I wanted to do was help someone that I loved. I know my father is probably turning in his grave right now. I was a disappointment to myself; I was a disappointment to him.

Chapter Twenty-Two

"It has been days, are you really still not talking to me?"

Silence

Sebastian posted my bail, but after he heard what the charge against me was he immediately stopped speaking to me. On one side I could see why he was upset about me marrying someone else. But on the other side, why did he care? It's not like our marriage was real for anything besides the paperwork and company events.

"I see that you are going to continue to be childish."

"WHAT TAY! What should I say to my wife after I find out that she has not only been cheating on me, but she went a step further and married the guy?"

"Cheating? You cannot be so egotistical that you believe that it is ok for you to screw a man in our house, on our couch, but when I do the same thing it is a crime against the sacredness of our marriage! WHO THE HELL ARE YOU TO JUDGE ME?"

"I can be upset because I never lied to you; I never sold you this dream. I have no earthly desire to be intimate with you. I asked you to marry me because a beautiful woman on your arm gets respect, but a man on your arm gets you stares and rumors. I have not changed from the beginning to now, but somewhere along the line you decided that you wanted something more. You decided that you wanted to change the arrangement so now I have to step in to clean up your mess while still selling the image of us being in a perfect relationship. I am going to have to stand on trial and say that I knew you just wanted to help a friend and that I love you beyond the way you decided to handle the situation. You have royally screwed up and now everyone knows it. At least I have the decency and respect for you to fuck my boyfriend in the privacy of my house. You said our but it's not our, this is MY HOUSE and everything in it belongs to ME!!! That includes you. I suggest that you get your shit together and remember what you are getting out of this deal. Now that your father is gone I am your only meal ticket. The next time you embarrass me like this you will find yourself on your ass, permanently staying at that shelter you seem to love so much nowadays."

Sebastian walked out of the house and slammed the door behind him. My father may have been my "meal ticket" before Sebastian but he was also my angel. I could talk to him about anything growing up, whenever he was home, and now I would clear out my bank account and Sebastian's just to talk to my father one more time.

I guess this was as good a time as any to finally read the letter that he left me. I opened it. It was short, sweet and to the point, just like always with my father. It did not take long to read, but to actually take in what was on the page would take some time. For now all I could think was wow. Even my wow was interrupted because Sebastian came back into the house and yelled for me to bring my ass. It was time for me to face the judge, the same judge that sentenced me to work in the shelter just a few months ago. I knew that my face was not one that he would be happy to see in his courtroom again.

Chapter Twenty-Three

"Did you miss my courtroom Dr. Thomas, is that why you are here again? I cannot fathom what would make someone who got off so easy to return here again so soon. Is this you mocking me? Are you taunting me for the decision I made the last time you were here?

"No your honor I am not."

"You are not what? You are not wasting time and resources due to your lack of belief that you are not above the law?"

"No your honor I am not."

"Well then please explain to me why you are in my courtroom for the second time in two months and if there is a record out there you are trying to break."

"Your honor I know that what I did was wrong but my intentions for doing it were right. Someone I cared about needed a life saving surgery and I had the ability to help him get it. While the way I chose to help was criminal what I actually did hurt no one."

"You don't think that your first husband Mr. Thomas was hurt by your actions? As someone who knew your father, God rest his soul, I know that he would have been hurt by your actions."

“I like to believe that my father would have initially been disappointed in me but would have then seen the sincere reasoning behind why I did it.”

“You might be right young lady. However you did in fact break the law and a punishment is needed. You will first pay for the work day of everyone in this courtroom today because it was your rash thinking that dragged all of us in today. Along with your time as a therapist at the homeless shelter, you will now be mandated to volunteer as a marriage counselor at the church on Sundays for the remainder of the year. Is there anything that you have to say for yourself?”

“No your honor.”

“Fine. Now in these cases the first marriage usually stays in place while the second one is annulled but as one final courtesy to your father I will allow you to decide which marriage you want to continue.”

“Do I have to decide right now?”

“Yes ma’am right now.”

I know that the judge may have thought that he was doing me a favor but in reality he was doing the exact opposite. When I made the suggestion to marry James I never thought about not being married to Sebastian in the process. I love James and would have done the same thing to save his life, but there was no way in hell that he could afford my lifestyle. Sebastian had become cold and distant over time but with him I could continue my shopping sprees and vacations without ever having to worry about the money being available to me. If I stayed married to Sebastian, he might still allow me to date James but I know that James would not go for that arrangement. I knew when we were in the hospital that he wanted all of me or none of me at all. Maybe there is a man out there like Sebastian who would support me like he does but not want to marry me.

"I am waiting."

Maybe there is another man like James out there for me who would be able to deal with the arrangement.

"I need your answer."

But I did not want a man like James, I want James.

"Who are you going to stay with Dr. Taylor?"

It would mean giving up everything that I was accustomed to.

"Who is it going to be?"

But the love I had for him was something I never had.

"Time is up!"

Some people have found love more than once in their lifetime; I could be one of those people.

"Enough of wasting everyone's time! Who is it going to be?"

I could feel every eyeball in the courtroom staring down at me waiting to see who I would chose. Love or comfort, comfort or love. I knew that once I gave my answer there would be no going back. I caught sight of Sebastian and James sitting in the corner, both just staring at me. Sebastian had this annoyed smirk on his face. James had sadness in his. It was like they both knew what I was going to say. I closed my eyes tight and tried to picture any place but here.

“If you do not give me your answer at this very instant, I will hold you in contempt of court!!”

“James!”

His name left my lips and I felt the entire dynamic of the room shift. What did I just do?

Chapter Twenty-Four

Nothing seemed real. Last week I signed the divorce papers to end my marriage with Sebastian and he wasted no time throwing me out and changing the locks on the house. For a week I had been living in the very shelter that was the vain of my existence months ago. Now it's the place I called home. The prenup that I signed when we got married clearly stated that I would get nothing if I divorced Sebastian and he saw to it that I got just that. The idea of me, ME being homeless seemed like such a bad soap opera twist, but it was my reality. The only thing that even felt remotely real was the pain from my decision. The reaction in the courtroom from Sebastian replayed in my head like a top 100 on the radio.

"What did you just say? What did she just say?"

"Mr. Thomas I am going to need for you to calm down."

"You want me to calm down your honor? She just threw away the last five years of my life for some common bum worth less than snot and you want me to calm down? I am clearly not the one who's not thinking right now."

"I understand your concerns Mr. Thomas but…"

"But what judge? You gave her the opportunity to choose and she made her decision. She chose to stand here and make a fool of me when all that I wanted to do was treat her the way she wanted to be treated; the way that I thought she deserved to be treated. Tay, you are nothing more than a conniving dependent whore. Why should I even be surprised? She is a user, has been her entire life. She used me until she found a bigger dick to ride. She used her father until he was in the grave, and now she is using you all."

"Do not mention my father! DO NOT DARE!"

"Is the truth too painful for you to handle now Tay?"

"You want to talk about the truth and it being too painful for me to handle? HOW WELL DO YOU HANDLE THE TRUTH SEBASTIAN?"

gavel bangs

"ORDER! I will have order in my courtroom!"

"The truth is my faithful loving husband Sebastian is nothing more than a lying manipulative jackass that spends his time INSIDE OF MEN! That is the truth and your honor the truth needed to be said to have your order."

What everyone was wearing and where they were standing was a blur, but the argument rang past through my ears into my very being, I never would have imagined that I would get a divorce let alone have a classless one as this. We had aired each other's dirty laundry for the world to see and there was nothing pretty about it.

Now I was left to deal with the aftermath of it all. I had lost my father, my husband, my bank account and my sanity as quickly as that…and for what? Is love really worth giving up everything that I care about? James and I had not even spoken since the courtroom fiasco. If he was ready to leave me too then this would have all been for nothing. I had been avoiding going back to the shelter now that I actually belonged in a place like that, but if I missed anymore days, my sentence would be lengthened. I am almost positive that they already knew what happened and that was partially why I was avoiding the shelter too. Now there was no more running.

Chapter Twenty-Five

I barely made it through the door before I heard Tori start.

"Look at what the cat drug in."

I thought that if I snuck in a little earlier I would beat the usual crowd. Turns out the early bird doesn't always catch the worm. Tori spared no time in letting it be known that she knew about my recent misfortune and I knew she would not be shy about discussing it.

Refusing to let my head hang, I casually said, "Hello to you too Tori."

She smiled a huge grin and eyes glared at me as she said, "Oh doc there's no need for formalities anymore, you're one of us!"

"I am not one of you."

"Let's not lie here. Let's not deny ourselves the view of such a beautiful display of irony. The very group that you looked down on, had disdain and called peasants, is now who you have become a part. We are now sitting at the same table, sharing the same scraps."

Chuckling and piercing her eyes at me she continued to remind me, "No hard feelings through doc, you can share my room if you don't mind the smell, what did you say we were? Oh yea, lazy, idiotic, inferior beings. Sorry we couldn't offer you a welcoming basket."

"You have no idea what you are talking about Tori."

Tori stepped closer to me, turned her nose up and said, "Maybe I don't, but that suit you have on looks mighty familiar."

I didn't think they would notice. Ashamed, I stared at the floor and thought to myself, she was right about everything. The suit looked familiar because Sebastian wouldn't even let me grab my clothes. I had been wearing the same suit for the last two days now. Though I was able to clean it and could afford a pack of underwear, there isn't much variety to a grey pencil skirt, silk blouse and double-breasted blazer.

Snapping out of my thoughts, I continued my way into our meeting room. I stood out like a sore thumb more than usual, every eye was on me. The further I stepped, the glares turned into stares. I guess Tori didn't keep the information to herself when she found out about my secret. I prepared myself for more comments and questions. The first coming from Craig.

"Oh how might they fall."

"Good afternoon to you as well Craig."

Lauren added, "If it means anything. I'm sorry about what happened to you doc."

"Thank you, Lauren. That means a lot."

Garrett didn't seem to take her empathy too well.

"Sorry to hear what happened to her? The pampered princess lost her throne, the same throne, she looked down on us from."

"I know that Garrett, but it still hurt her."

"You should feel sorry for her husband, well both husbands. Or is it the ex-husband or current, which one is it doc?"

Irritated but trying to stay calm, I breathed and responded, "You all can make all the jokes you want, but I knew what I was risking when I decided on my decision. I do not regret any of it. I care about both Sebastian and James."

Garrett continued with the questions, "If you care about them, why did you deceive them? "

A long sigh let out as I explained, "The issue was not in deceiving them; I was deceiving myself. I married James to help him but a part of it was to help myself."

"Are you trying to make it better because if so, you are sucking at it! You just sound more and more selfish."

"No, I am not trying to make it better, I'm trying to be honest. I care about Sebastian, but I married him out of the comforts he had to offer me. It was a business deal honestly. With James it's deeper. I married him knowing the risks because I love him and would give anything to help him." Before I knew what I was saying, I had the most honest moment and came to the realization, " I never would have seen myself as the girl who gives up all she has for love, or who would have thought that someone with so little, could offer me something I didn't know I was missing, love. James warms me; it sounds cliché but he makes me a better person. He nurtures my inner being and helps me blossom into the woman I've always longed to be. I loved Sebastian with my mind and for what he had to offer me; I love James with my heart and soul"

I heard the familiar warm voice that I had longed for the past few days, "Do you really mean that?"

Turning to see James, I realized I had been so engrossed with explaining myself to everyone that I didn't notice when he walked into the room. It was the first time that I had seen him since the trial. My body stiffened and my smile disappeared as I felt my heart race and temperature rise. I had longed for his voice, his touch but he had gone. At that moment I wanted to kick him in the balls for disappearing after I chose him. I felt my body pulse as I lashed out.

"I did mean it at first, but since your disappearing act I have been questioning how I could be so stupid to give up everything for a man who didn't even stick around! I guess I can only blame myself for putting my life in the hands of a man who would forget his own name if he missed a pill. And I use the term man loosely just so you know."

The look of sorrow came across his face as he stepped closer, "Taylor, hush!."

"No! I will not! You made me love you, you made me choose you and you left me." I felt myself yelling, "Fuck you."

His eyes narrowed and jaw clenched, "Taylor shut up."

I continued... "Do not tell me what to do James! You no longer have that option –"

Cutting me off and yelling, "Taylor! Shut the hell up!"

Stunned, I went silent. I had heard James yell when he was going through an episode, but never at me. It was stern and forceful; it scared me. No matter how scared I was, I wouldn't let it be shown. I felt like crying, but refused. I wasn't going to let him add to the river of tears I cried when searching the streets for him, worried about him, but also worried about myself because I had nowhere to go. Remembering the breathing techniques he showed me, I inhaled and exhaled. " So are you yelling at me now?"

His hazel eyes piercing at me as he said, " No. I am raising my voice so that you understand how serious I am about what I'm about to say, so that you hear me loud and clear. I also want you to know I apologize."

"Apologize?" Feeling my temperature rise, I snapped. "Now after I literally lose everything you want to apologize? I needed you, you walked away from it all. But what hurt the most was you walked away from me! You cannot apologize for that."

"Good because that is not what I want to apologize for."

"Well what on earth are you wasting my time for?"

James stepped even closer to me. He was merely inches from my face now; my anger turned into being anxious as he fiddled with his jacket pocket. He was no longer mad and his tone had softened. "I want to apologize for not asking you to marry me before you asked me. I want to apologize for allowing you to give up everything for someone like me. I think it also helps to apologize for stealing a few of your ex-husbands watches to pay for this." I froze and for the first time in my life, I was at a loss for words. He got down on one knee, held my hand tenderly and continued, "I will probably never be a millionaire. I will probably never be able to give you the lifestyle that you are accustomed too. I recognize that, but I have been scratching and saving just to have a second chance in life. You are my second chance. I disappeared so I could go pick up a fifteen year old Honda and sign a lease on a one bedroom apartment. You are my wife on paper, but I'm now asking you to be my wife physically and spiritually. I may not have a single sane bone left in my body, but with you everything seems okay. I love you and I apologize for taking so long to say it. Taylor will you make me the happiest person in this loony bin and continue to be my wife?"

I was screaming yes in my head, but the words refused to form in my mouth. I flashed back to James leaving me. My expression turned into concern and he continued.

Stop thinking so loudly Taylor. I know that you are afraid of repeating the same relationship you had, but I'm not Sebastian and I will not leave you again. Right now, right here, I am promising you that I am in this for the long run."

I heard Lauren say, "Look doc if you don't take him I will."

I had completely forgotten that we were surrounded by people. I smiled brightly and said. "I do."

He slid the sterling silver, solitaire white, sapphire ring on my finger, got up and embraced me. I felt so alive. It's difficult to admit, but I felt more in that moment then I had in a long time. How could I continue to judge and look down on everyone in this room. There was nothing in my past that could even slightly suggest that I would be in this moment right now. The world didn't care about the private schools I attended, the designer labels that once flooded my closet. Everyone else in the world saw that I had failed; I am a person just like everyone else. I am not exempt from pain, joy, or hardships.

Made in the USA
Columbia, SC
21 July 2018